THE RECOVERY
OF FAMILY LIFE

THE RECOVERY
OF FAMILY LIFE

BY
ELTON TRUEBLOOD
AND
PAULINE TRUEBLOOD

HARPER & BROTHERS
Publishers · New York

Library of Congress catalogue card number: 53-8375

To Martin *and* Arnold *and* Samuel *and* Elizabeth, *who came into our home involuntarily, to* Margaret *and* Caroline, *who came by choice, and to* Leona Boyd, *able cook and housekeeper, who set one of us free to write*

Contents

Preface

SINCE the time of Socrates it has been an accepted part of Western wisdom that, in matters of social organization, it is necessary to know what is right before we can know what is wrong. Insofar as man is reasonable, the intelligent way to begin is to consider first the end. The only reason why a physician can diagnose the nature of an illness is that he already has a vision of what a really well body is. "It is the whole definition and dignity of man," said Chesterton, "that in social matters we must actually find the cure before we find the disease." Unless we know that there *is* a target and unless we have a fairly clear idea of its location, it is surely nonsense to talk about *missing* it.

In the problem of the recovery of family life this common-sense approach is as necessary as it is rare. Because the difficulties we encounter are more profound than they appear, it is especially important that we start at the right place. We need many books on the economics of the family, on sexual behavior and on the details of domestic education, but these questions are secondary to the central question of what a family ought to be. The economic and physiological questions are important, but the philosophical question comes first.

This book is an effort to deal with the recovery of family life at the right place. The intention is to depict an enduring ideal which is practically realizable and which, we believe, has such inherent attractiveness that its very depiction becomes a factor in the recovery and development of what is most precious in our civilization as well as an antidote to some of our most distressing ills.

Some subjects may be considered in detachment, but not this one. For a book, with such a purpose to be worthy of attention it must be written by people who have not only thought about the central subject, but have also tested it in practice. A family book should be a family matter. That is why this book has not been written by one of us alone. What we present, therefore, is fundamentally a *witness*, because we believe that such a witness is what so many troubled persons in our age now need. We have written against the background of a happy home, marked by close and enduring affection on the part of all of its members. By this we are willing to be judged.

Though in most areas of human experience we tend to listen to those who have been successful in the enterprises which they discuss, our generation has shown, in late years, a curious tendency to listen, in regard to the family, to those without experience or to those who have failed. Perhaps the time has now come when public taste may change in this regard. In any case we have been mindful, in all of our writing, that actions speak louder than words, and we have written nothing that has not proved applicable to our own home for twenty-nine years.

We are grateful to Southwestern University for the opportunity to use again a few sentences from the Willson Lectures at that institution which appeared under the title, *The Common Ventures of Life.*

E. T. — P. T.

Earlham College, June, 1953

THE RECOVERY
OF FAMILY LIFE

CHAPTER I

The Withering Away of the Family

We replace home education by social.
Communist Manifesto

AS WE plunge deeper into the undeclared civil war of the planet, which waxes and wanes, but does not thereby cease, we tend to exaggerate, at many points, the differences between the thought and practice which characterize human life on the two sides of the iron curtain. The really frightening thought, however, is that of the degree to which the two sides are *similar*. In spite of the different labels, we are more like the Russians than we realize or choose to admit. In no area of our experience is the developing similarity more disturbing than that of family life. The sobering truth is that, in our conception of the family and its place in a total society, we are producing, without considered and conscious intent, much that the Russian planners have achieved by deliberate ideological emphasis. We are doing by neglect much that the Marxists have done by social planning.

The *Communist Manifesto* made the attack on family loyalty perfectly clear. The *Manifesto* spoke of "The bour-

13

geois claptrap about the family and education, about the hallowed co-relation of parent and child." That the family, as developed through Judeo-Christian influence would come to an end with the completed revolution was vigorously asserted. "The bourgeois family," says the *Manifesto,* "will vanish as a matter of course when its complement (prostitution) vanishes, and both will vanish with the vanishing of capital." The main shift which the communist authors envisaged was from the family unit to larger social agencies. The teaching was that children belong primarily to the state and not primarily to the home.

We cannot understand modern Marxist doctrine unless we know something of the degree to which it has embraced militant feminism. The basic idea is that men and women must be treated in identical ways except for some special provision for pregnancy and nursing. The notion of a woman as the center of a home, giving it peace, order and continuous affection, is considered a quaint bourgeois prejudice which the emancipated or "scientific" modern will give up as soon as he is awakened to the true situation. Women must, therefore, be expected to work in factories, in offices and on farms, exactly as men do. They will earn in the same way and they will be willing to give up the antiquated notion that children are better trained in homes than they are in public institutions. The shift of the cultural center of gravity from the home to public institutions was explained by Engels in the following statement:

It is already clear at this point that the emancipation of woman, her equalisation with man, is and remains impossible so long as the woman is excluded from the productive work of society and remains restricted to private household work. The emancipation of woman first becomes possible when she is able on an extensive, social scale, to participate in production, and household work claims her attention only to an insignificant extent. And this for the first time has been made possible by large scale industry, which not only admits women's labor over a wide range, but absolutely demands it, and also strives to transform private household work more and more into a public industry.[1]

It is important to remember that the breakup of the family is not incidental, but central to official communist ideology. This was one of the ideas on which Lenin insisted most strongly. He described the public nursery, which sets the mother free from the burden of constant care of the young children, and thus enables her to earn an independent livelihood, as being the "germ cell of the communist society." Communist ideology thus sought to carry to the ultimate conclusion the familiar feminist ideal of the nineteenth century. We can understand and even appreciate this conception as a violent reaction against the former subjection and extreme domesticity of women, but this is no justification, inasmuch as the one extreme may be quite as unlovely as the other.

The official Marxist doctrine, all along, has been that the home, when it is given social priority and real importance, involves *parasitism*. The unemployed woman is declared to be a parasite, roughly comparable to the industrialist who

[1] Friedrich Engels, "The Origin of the Family, Private Property and the State," *A Handbook of Marxism*, pp. 318, 319. Engels, after the death of Marx in 1883, wrote this work, making use of Marx's notes. Marx had intended to write on the subject.

is guilty of profiting by directing to his own use what is known as surplus value. Of course it follows, if the unproductiveness of home life can be demonstrated, that families, as ordinarily organized, represent economic waste. Since there are fully as many females as males, the "emancipation of women" practically doubles the labor power at one stroke. At the same time the state wins a great victory of another kind, in that the task of propagandizing all minds is made far easier when the center of education becomes public rather than private. Education which is "an instrument of propaganda for the communist regeneration of society"[2] is made easier if the family does not compete or interfere. A woman who works all day in the factory or office will not have the extra energy to engage seriously in her time-honored educational task or to share in it with her husband. All of her surplus energy will be required for the domestic duties which necessarily occupy the margin of her time.

As early as 1920 Lenin reported great success in his crucial enterprise, especially in the following words:

The Government of the proletarian dictatorship, together with the Communist Party and the trade unions, is, of course, leaving no stone unturned in the effort to overcome the backward ideas of men and women, to destroy the old uncommunist psychology. . . . We are establishing communal kitchens and public eating-houses, laundries and repairing shops, infant asylums, kindergartens, children's homes, educational institutes of all kinds. In short we are seriously carrying out the demand of our programme for the transference of the economic and educational functions of the separate household to society.

[2] Laski's phrase.

As is well known, a great deal of sexual promiscuity was permitted or even encouraged in the early days of the Revolution, because the older loyalties, especially the religious ones, were breaking down, but the time soon came when the leaders realized that such promiscuity was disastrous. In the earliest days of the new order, sexual intercourse was often considered a wholly personal matter, having no moral or social implications, and was sometimes compared to drinking a glass of water. But as early as 1921 Lenin denounced strenuously the "glass of water" theory on the grounds that intercourse has social results, which the drinking of water does not have. He called the theory "uncommunist" and called for a stern self-control in the interests of the new society. "The Revolution," he said, "demands concentration. . . . And so, I repeat, no weakening, no waste, no destruction of forces. Self-control, self-discipline, not slavery, not even in love. . . . Such questions are part of the woman question."

The Russians have retreated ideologically on the marriage aspect of what Lenin called "the woman question," but not essentially on the *family* aspect. They have made divorce less easy than it was at first, but they have not retreated from the belief in universal employment, with the consequent diminution of the importance of the home. What they fear is not marriage or even a neo-Puritanism, in regard to sex, but rather the cultural independence of the family unit. This fact is very important for any serious consideration of our own cultural predicament in the life of the West.

"The state," said Engels, "will not be 'abolished,' it will

wither away." This is the classic statement of a well-known communist doctrine, but the conception involved is broader than this particular application. Other institutions besides the state may wither away even if the state does not, and of these the family is a conspicuous example. In the life of the West, and particularly of America, there is no self-conscious or concerted attack on the family, as there has been in Russia since the beginning of the Revolution, but harm may nevertheless come. Our danger arises, not from direct attack, but from a multitude of separate factors, no one of which is sufficient, of itself, to destroy the family, but which, in their combination, make an impact which is truly terrible to observe or to contemplate.

One factor is the uprootedness of people in the industrial age. Hundreds of thousands live in trailer camps or in other temporary quarters where the stabilizing factors in family life are almost wholly absent. The people who exist in this way, moving from one well-paid job to another, often have a good deal of ready money, but they miss almost entirely the sense of belonging that can be so stabilizing. We have millions who have no real stake in the community and no membership in a group whose approbation is highly valued. Uprooted men and women do not take the same pride in family success, and when people cease to care, the family naturally goes to pieces.

Ease of divorce, a lowered sense of the importance of sexual morality and the general dislocations of the postwar period have combined to put the family in jeopardy, but it is the subtler forces which count for most in this regard. Of all the disintegrating factors the chief is the loss of the sense of meaning of what a family ought to be. Our basic failure is not the failure to live up to a standard that is accepted, but rather the failure to keep the standard clear! The majority who live in settled homes rather than trailer camps may be uprooted also, because they have lost confidence in the essential sacredness of the family as the basic unit of society.

The central question is the question of priority. Many Americans, like many Russians, are willing to permit the existence of homes, since people must eat and sleep somewhere, but they allow the dignity of the home to be lost by degrees, because they do not resist the tendency to make the home chiefly an *adjunct* to other institutions. Actually, the family is so important in our total life that the shoe ought to be on the other foot. A good case can be made for the thesis that the various social organizations should be judged by what they do to the *family*. The club, the school, and other agencies ought to exist to serve the family far more than the family exists to serve them, because these outside institutions are *instrumental* while the family is *terminal* in value. The family is an end in itself because it is actually the only place in our world where the loving fellowship, which is the purpose of all our striving, is actually demonstrated. A symptom of our sickness is our strange tendency to reverse the order of value.

It is part of the paradox of contemporary life in America that some of the greatest dangers to the family come from institutions inspired by noble aims, bent on lifting of the level of civilization, yet failing at the central point. A conspicuous example of this is the modern school. Much of the contemporary educational philosophy is really totalitarian, though, of course, it does not claim to be so. The school proposes to take over many of the functions formerly associated with the home as well as many historically belonging to the church. Often the school sets itself up as the teacher of morals as well as the director of the entire social and recreational experience. The father of the family may be so old-fashioned that he would be willing to give a few nights to reading aloud in the family circle, but school life is so overorganized that it is almost impossible to find a free evening. Some schools now play more than twenty basketball games in a season and great pressure is put on all students to attend all games, as a matter of school loyalty. Then there are the plays, with the interminable rehearsals, the dances, the selling of tickets, the drives, the entertainments.

The consequence of all this is that a terrible onus is put upon the parent who resists. In one large school a visiting psychologist was brought by the school administration to address the Parent-Teacher Association, the burden of his message being that parents who keep their children away from any of the social activities sponsored by the high school are thereby harming their children, possibly irreparably.

The strange thing about all this emphasis is that so few seem to realize how presumptuous it is. In short, without calling ourselves Marxists at all, we have actually adopted a great part of Marxist ideology at a crucial point. In the words of the *Communist Manifesto,* quoted at the beginning of this chapter, "We replace home education by social." We have so much lost our pride that we do not even resent the presumption of the "expert" who tells us blandly that he can handle our children better than we can. We build our lovely homes, at great sacrifice, and then tolerate meekly a situation in which nearly all of the child's waking hours are spent outside its sheltering walls.

There are some who have declared that the existence of television reverses this trend away from the home, but the judgment is premature. Home life is not really restored to its priority by the simple expedient of turning one of its rooms into a theater in which people sit in semi-darkness and without conversation or other creative enterprise. The recovery of family life is not a problem so simple that it can be solved by the introduction of a new technological device. Undoubtedly television does tend to keep some members of the family at home, but the question of the beneficence of this experience remains unanswered. If our major choice is between separation from the home and hypnosis in the living room we are in a bad way indeed. Those who stay at home only for television are still in the theater, spiritually.

It cannot be doubted that many parents aid and foster the tendencies which take the children out of the home or keep them passively occupied in it. They welcome the television program, whatever the unconscious sinister influences involved in it, because the program keeps the children quiet for awhile. Likewise many parents welcome the Saturday motion picture at the neighborhood theater, however vulgar, because it keeps the children out of the house. Quite obviously it is easier to patronize commercial entertainment than to think up profitable family enterprises or to give them the time and effort they require when they are carried out.

There is no doubt that many parents send their children to Sunday School, on Sunday morning, not merely because they are eager for religious instruction, but partly because the practice gives the father a little peace while he reads the oversize newspaper. The fact that children are sent rather than *accompanied* is soon obvious to them and helps to account for a general decline in attendance during adolescence.

The adults of the modern family find the real centers of their lives outside the home almost as much as the children do. The father comes home from work, eats his dinner, and then, becoming restless, goes out to the club house or to the tavern. He feels that he needs some relaxation. In similar fashion countless women find their steady satisfactions in bridge clubs or other extradomestic undertakings. When such is true of both fathers and mothers as well as children we are bound to arrive sooner or later at the spectacle of the atomized family, already experienced by many in varying degrees. The chief social forces are centrifugal, with the result that there is a marked contrast between the beautifully furnished houses, which the home magazines encourage, and what goes on inside them. Our difficulty lies not primarily in our domestic architecture; neither does it lie in our equipment; it lies chiefly in our poverty of spirit.

In no phase of our family life is the similarity of pattern on the two sides of the iron curtain more obvious than in the public employment of women. The chief differences

are differences of degree and of the reasons for the practice, but many of the harmful effects are essentially the
same in both areas of the world. The chief reasons why
wives and mothers in America seek employment are three,
economic, ideological and *personal*. Sometimes these motives are combined.

The economic motives cover a wide range. Sometimes
the earning of the mother is a necessity for survival, as
is obviously the case when the woman is a widow or the
wife of a husband who is handicapped, incompetent or
faced with financial calamity. In numerous instances, however, the economic motive is far less compelling and
amounts to little more than a desire for a higher standard
of living.

It might be supposed that current high wages in America would practically eliminate the threat to family life
which comes from economic strain, but this result has by
no means come to pass. High as wages are, there has been
no marked diminution in multiple earning within a
single family unit. Even more damaging is the practice,
among men, of accepting two jobs, with the result that
fathers and children almost never see one another, for
the father is away evenings as well as on week-ends. A survey
in one great city is astonishing in that it shows that 35
per cent of the employed men had double employment.
The short working week, looked for so eagerly as a means
of providing creative leisure and time for home life, has,
for thousands, become only an opportunity for longer
hours of employment and greater earning in the effort to
keep up with the economic rat race, made more intense

by the twin factors of the inflation of our money and the increased desire for ever more expensive objects. This desire is greatly stimulated by the constant and highly appealing advertising of what are essentially luxury products. Increasingly, what were formerly luxuries are now felt as genuine requirements, especially necessary in the maintenance of social standing at some particular level.

The growing tendency for great corporations, such as the chain grocery stores, to operate seven days a week is a threat to family life. The persons employed are, of course, given at least one day each week to be at home, but usually the days are so staggered that it is almost impossible for family occasions to be planned and carried out. The situation in which the father is home each evening, and for a long week-end, seems to many of our people a beautiful dream, but practically impossible for them to enjoy in practice.

Many careful surveys of the employment of mothers have been made, but one of the most thorough as well as one of the most recent, is that of Wichita, Kansas.[3] The Wichita survey gives contemporary support to the national findings made public by The Children's Bureau of Washington, D. C. Important facts revealed by the Wichita survey are that 20 per cent of all children under seventeen have employed mothers. Since there is no significant difference between the size of families of employed and unemployed mothers, this means that in one family out of

[3] The survey was made by virtue of a grant from the Elizabeth McCormick Memorial Fund of Chicago. It was conducted by the Community Planning Council of Wichita.

every five, where there are children of school age or below, the mother is employed outside the home.

Many devices are used to care for the children while both parents are away. A grandmother or other relative is the most widely used substitute for the mother, but in many situations these are not available because they do not live nearby. The absence of close relatives is one of the human prices we pay for our migratory industrial economy. Some children are left with strangers for pay, some are left in day nurseries and others are left to shift for themselves. Almost 20 per cent of the children of employed mothers were found to be wholly without supervision before and after school. Several hundred children were found to be in a position where they had to shift for themselves during the evening meal, early evening and all or part of the night. The youngest of these were eight years old.

It is important to realize that nearly all mothers who are interviewed tend to put the situation of their children in the best possible light, because they do not wish to be accused of neglect. Accordingly, we may be sure that the actual effect in the lives of children is worse than factual reports indicate. The worst effects, having to do with the child's sense of insecurity, are intangible and largely unconscious, but this phase of the withering away of the family is undoubtedly building up a sad human harvest for the future.

Most parents who operate on the basis of double earning report that they do so from economic necessity, though this is, of course, a term of high ambiguity. In many cases the need is obviously genuine, especially when there has been catastrophic illness with consequent debt. Many are trying desperately to get together enough money to provide a down payment on a house of their own while others are trying to keep up payments on a car or a television set. Only a few of the young employed mothers are widows. Eighty-five per cent of those employed are not heads of households.

When we consider the human price of this increasingly accepted social pattern of double earning, we usually stress the harmful effects upon children or the hardening of the mothers, but the effect upon the adult men may be quite as important in the long run. Once men took great pride in being able to provide for their families and resented any implication that a second pay check was needed, but now many men welcome whatever help the wife can give. What we are witnessing is a feminization of men, a psychological development independent of physical characteristics. In modern life a man often goes from dependence on one woman to dependence upon another. Thus the man is cheated of his basis of self-respect and the woman is cheated in that she never has the sense of security which a strong man gives. In this situation it is hard to know how much is cause and how much is effect; the wife has to earn because the man does not provide sufficiently, but his very failure to provide may come partly because of a social pattern which undermines his self-respect.

We do not claim to have any easy answers to these problems, but we are very sure of two things. First, those of us who do not face this economic and social problem must be very tender toward those who do, and, second, we must understand clearly the human harm which comes as the family withers away at important levels in our society. Only as we understand the loss will we have the incentive adequate to make us use our imagination to reverse the process of decay.

The ideological motive for the employment of married women may now seem a bit dated, but nevertheless continues strong in some areas. Many women are very ambitious to prove that they can compete with men in men's fields, but they are not willing to give up the opportunity to have families, so they try to perform the miracle of carrying on two full-time occupations at once. "I do not deny," says Chesterton, "that women have been wronged and even tortured; but I doubt if they were ever tortured so much as they are tortured now by the absurd modern attempt to make them domestic empresses and competitive clerks at the same time."[4]

The third motive for the paid employment of married women is easily understandable and very widespread in its effect. This is the personal one, according to which women leave the circle of the home out of boredom and loneliness. The young woman, taking care daily of the needs of little boys and girls and answering innumerable questions when she is physically tired, begins to envy the life of her husband and of her unmarried sisters. Their lives seem so attractive by contrast. They chat endlessly with other adults, they go out for mid-morning coffee, they work in

[4] G. K. Chesterton, *What's Wrong with the World* (New York: Dodd, Mead and Company, 1910), p. 160.

groups and they have the excitement of daily transportation. It is very easy for the tired mother to romanticize about other occupations, particularly those in which a person can use her mind. Escape can come by employment, she thinks, and the children won't suffer much because the extra money will pay for their care.

At this point it is easy to combine the second motive with the third. The mother feels, perhaps justifiably, that our present culture accords no real prestige or distinction to what a mother does in her home, but she understands very well that honor comes to those who succeed in business or the professions. Many of the powerful opinion makers of our time are conspiring against the woman who operates at the center of the home, helping to make her despise her own role in society. Several of the photo magazines have presented recently highly glamorized scenes from the lives of women who are engaged in business or some professional work all week and who graciously give their week-ends to their families. The mother who has finally sent her three little ones to school by eight o'clock and then has sat down to read the beautiful magazine may be pardoned if she feels a touch of envy of the glamor mothers in the advertising game.

The test of any pattern of life is what it does to the people involved. In this case we are concerned both with the effect on married couples and the effect on children. Inevitably it is the children who suffer most. Some men may not resent a situation in which they are deprived of the satisfaction of being the adequate breadwinner of a family and some may actually encourage the wife's participation in earning, but the children are not usually consulted. Some of them do not know what they are missing, because they have never experienced any other arrangement, but they are harmed nevertheless.

The harm in the situation is that of always coming to the empty house with no one there to welcome the one who returns. Character and temperament are formed far more by such intangibles than they are by overt teaching. The woman who thinks that she has a dull job, staying at home and doing dull work, may, in fact, be performing an amazing service by the psychological stability she provides. Because numerous fathers must, in the nature of the case, be away a great deal in the accomplishment of their needed tasks, it is all the more important that a center of stability be maintained. The notion that this can be done adequately by hired servants is grotesque. How lacking in self-confidence a mother must be who supposes that the steady impact upon character can be better performed by persons she hires to do the job while someone hires her to do another job. It would take a very strange ideology to justify such a procedure, yet many accept it uncritically as a matter of course.

The usual assumption is that mothers can be employed outside the home with no consequent harm to the children because of the use of nursery schools. This is really part of the collectivist philosophy, strikingly similar to that enunciated by Lenin, and now has very wide vogue in America, but there are at least two things wrong with it, however fashionable it may be. In the first place, it is far from self-evident that children are better off under what is known as expert social care. They get some advantages thereby, but they miss others that may be more important. It was impressive to watch the late Ray Lyman Wilbur, when the collectivist fashion was proposed, as it normally was in the marriage courses in the university of which he was president, and to hear him say in his Lincolnesque manner, "I've never noticed that children brought up in orphan asylums are so much superior to children brought up in families."

The second defect of the collectivist philosophy of child training is that, when all the members of the family are home together at night, the little children who are naturally hungering for loving interest are given only the tag end of the parental day. Domestic work must be done somehow, even in Russia, and the fact that it is supposedly done by both father and mother as equal partners does not eliminate it. What chance do children have when both parents are not only tired from the day's work outside, but also have to do all the day's housework in their supposedly leisure hours? Anyone who has witnessed many such scenes knows that they are far from the loveliness of the Marxist Utopian dream. It is the right of little children to have individual love all day long and to have more than the tag ends of affection. But this situation will not change until the family is seen as an institution so precious that men and women will sacrifice something, even in excitement and personal expression, in order to maintain it.

The tide of ideological fashion seems still to be moving in the direction of universal employment outside the home. It is not uncommon to find great factory and commercial establishments where there are more female than male employees. There are the so-called "chicken farms," offices in which endless rows of women are busy pecking away all day long. The sight is somehow very depressing. *En masse* they seem desexed, like the workers in the beehive. They are potential queens who have missed their vocation. Each *could* be pictured at the center of a home, making an island of peace and order in the confusion and strain of our day, but instead she runs an adding machine or files addresses in a noisy room filled with women.

The chain of disaster is clear. The homes devoid of regular or continuous care lead directly to insecurity and delinquency on the part of the young. These in turn set up homes where a similar pattern is demonstrated. How shall we break this vicious chain? Before we can break it we need to know the nature of the trouble. Part of the trouble is, of course, economic, but by no means all. A good share of the trouble is moral and, if we go beyond the surface, most of it may be. One of the chief reasons why so many habitations are not homes is that other things are prized more.

The moral aspect of the decay of family life is obvious in the relations of the sexes to each other. There are, of course, millions of families in which there is lifelong marital fidelity, but it is frightening to realize that these may now constitute only a minority of our population. If the figures given out by the Kinsey Report are reliable, it may be estimated that more than half of the adult population of contemporary America shows, in practice, only slight respect for marital fidelity. What seems to have occurred is that great numbers consider sexual morality something quaint and meaningless for our time. Like the Russians in the first flush of the Revolution, many accept the "drink of water" conception and believe adultery a trivial affair, especially in the light of the fact that modern inventions make unlikely the permanent effects that have sometimes served as deterrents in the past.

Part of the trouble lies in the fact that so much of the idea of sanctity is gone. Easy divorce and quick remarriage, after the Nevada model, mean that marriage is seen primarily as a private convenience rather than a sacred undertaking. C. C. Zimmerman, in his Harvard study, *Family and Civilization*, perhaps the most thorough work of the kind now in existence, puts the matter tersely when he says, "In other words the family is considered *de facto*, a private contract of a very brittle nature and as having not even a mild public significance."[5] It ought to be clear that the present withering of the family is exactly what we should expect in the light of the absence of a generally accepted philosophy which would support the sanctity of marriage. The people who rush to Reno are not doing the surprising thing; they are doing the wholly natural thing, given their presuppositions. It is at this point that Zimmerman's analysis is both helpful and clear. "The religious and moral agents," he writes, "which once supported their systems of familism are largely out of favor with the masses or are inwardly corrupted by lack of knowledge of their real functions in society."[6]

The secular atomism of the modern family makes three

[5] Harper & Brothers, 1947, p. 760.
[6] *Ibid*, p. 762.

fundamental mistakes. First, it sees marriage as mere contract, second, it understands marriage as a private affair, and third, it adopts a philosophy of self-expression and empty freedom which rules out the claims of self-sacrifice and self-control.

As marriage becomes less sacred, and divorce more acceptable, many reach the facile conclusion that easy divorce is thereby justified. This is akin to the curious reasoning based on the Kinsey Report of sexual behavior, to the effect that infractions of the moral code are no longer evil because many commit them. But what a curiously naïve logic to conclude that right and wrong can be discovered by statistical method. Homosexual practices are not justified by the revelation, which nobody doubted, that a good many persons have temptations in this direction. What is commonly practiced is often wrong, in spite of its popularity.

Another phase of the moral problem of the family concerns the attitude of children toward their parents. The revolt against parental authority has gone so far that many young people have lost both politeness and a sense of respect. A characteristic college boy, when he heard the phrase "elders and betters," replied, "I have no betters." This superficial notion of equality where equality does not exist is the logical result of the doctrine of empty freedom, according to which each person is encouraged to follow self-expression and resist any limitation on personal decision. Naturally the family suffers first in this situation since the major values of family life, whether we realize it or not, depend upon a great degree of limitation on the personal action of the individual. The doctrine of freedom as popularly held and sometimes practiced leads not only to easy divorce, when marriage becomes galling, but likewise to a refusal, on the part of children, to accept the responsibilities which membership entails. In so far as freedom of action is seen as the primary or sole value, the family is progressively atomized and consequently destroyed.

We know a great deal about our diseased time when we see the growth of interest in abnormal psychology. In many universities the courses in abnormal behavior are the most popular of all courses in psychology, while numerous marriage courses achieve popularity because of their reputation for emphasis on sex. Apparently the undisguised pornography of the books in the drug stores is not sufficient to satisfy the demand. But what widespread futility there must be which causes people to turn to such substitutes! The bizarre interests are symptoms of a deep failure to find something positive and satisfying at the center of our lives.

A contemporary notion that is almost as popular as it is absurd is the belief that the good life can be produced by the simple expedient of spreading sex knowledge. The fatuousness of this belief ought to be obvious when we reflect upon the fact that some of the most ruthless of sexual offenders are those whose sexual information must be immense. More than knowledge is necessary for the good life, whatever the area of experience. Knowledge is *necessary*, but it certainly is not *sufficient*.

It is likewise not enough to go to the other extreme and

take a stiff line in regard to the remarriage of divorced persons. This is only one incident in a larger whole. What we need is a far wider view in which we refuse to concentrate merely on the relations of husband and wife and give our attention even more to the relations between parent and child. We make much of the break of affection which leads to divorce, but we have not given adequate attention to the break between parents and children, for which there is no handy common noun. What we need is an ideological transformation in regard to the family, including a new sense of motivation.

Fortunately, there are still thousands, perhaps millions of good families in America where the bonds of affection are kept strong, but not even these are free from the danger of the withering processes around them. Only by vigilance can the valued life we already have be kept and only by careful thought can its scope be increased. As the major threat to the life of the family lies in our ideas and convictions, so it is in this same area that our hope for a better future likewise lies. Can we recover or produce a conception of family life so intrinsically appealing that it makes us dissatisfied with the withering of the family in either the Russian or the Western style? That we *can* is the thesis of this book, and to the delineation of such a conception we turn in the next chapter.

CHAPTER II

The Idea of the Family

> Therefore shall a man leave his father and his mother, and shall cleave unto his wife: and they shall be one flesh.
>
> GENESIS 2:24

THE existence of the family rests on many foundations, some of which are strictly biological. Two biological facts are very important in this regard. The first is that the human being feels sexual desire at all seasons of the year, standing, in this regard, in strong contrast to many other creatures, as, for example, the deer, who experiences this desire at one season only. This is one of the reasons why there is some tendency for a man and a woman to live together permanently. The second important biological fact is that of the long period of helplessness and need on the part of the human young. Man's young mature very slowly. If they are to live at all they must be cared for a long time and the fact that they are highly educable tends to increase this period of dependence. Man's need of education, both mental and moral, is different in kind from anything known in subhuman nature and demands appropriate institutions for its development, the chief of these being the home.

The family is the effort to satisfy successfully a great variety of human needs, both physical and spiritual. As such, we need to be reminded of the fact that it is "the most successful of human institutions." This point is made in a telling manner by George C. Homans of Harvard University, in his exciting book, *The Human Group*, and elaborated as follows:

We do not mean to imply against the evidence, that all marriages are happy, but that marriage must fulfill a universal human need, if we can judge from the fact that the nuclear family, consisting of an approved association between a man, at least one woman, and their children is found as a recognizable unit in every known society.[1]

A great deal of the earlier anthropological speculation, such as was popular at the beginning of our century, has ceased to be impressive. Especially doubtful, in the light of further study in the field, is the notion that men and women, in primitive society, had promiscuous sexual relations as an accepted practice and that the children were brought up by the group as a whole rather than by particular couples. Professor Nimkoff has this kind of theorizing in mind when he says, "Some of it is ingenuous, much of it is fascinating, but all of it is speculative."[2] So deep rooted does the family now seem that Homans can

[1] New York: Harcourt, Brace & Co., 1950, p. 190.
[2] Meyer Francis Nimkoff, *The Family*, edited by William F. Ogburn (Boston: Houghton Mifflin Co., 1934), p. 117.

boldly say, "It may be that men have lived in families as long as men have been men."[3]

The institution of the family is such an enormous success in the sense that it endures through change, that we may be sure of its continuation in some form. But the danger is that it may continue in some withered form rather than in full health. Because there are several different forms which family life can take, we must use intelligence to choose among them and guide our course accordingly.

Many different patterns of human life are possible. Though we now take the organization of the human race in family units for granted, mere survival might be possible in several other ways. Instead of housing human beings in small groups, consisting in each case of father, mother and the children of that pair, we could house them in vast dormitories. We could have one dormitory for men, one for women and another for children. Something like this has actually been tried in various Utopian social experiments, made up of small colonies, and the essence of this was seriously advocated by Plato, so far as the guardians of his ideal state were concerned. Some such system is almost universal for those who have, for some reason, lost their freedom and now reside in prisons or concentration camps.

When modern man lives in family units, he does this not by necessity, but by choice. He *could* survive otherwise, but he realizes that survival value is not enough; he asks not merely how he can survive, but how he can live *well*. It is the almost unanimous judgment of mankind that the

[3] *Op. cit.*, p. 191.

best life is that which makes family living the basic unit. Much as we admire the powerful mentality of Plato, we do not really admire the Spartan pattern which influenced him, nor do we take seriously his proposals in *The Republic,* for eliminating family loyalty at certain levels of society. Students agree that the Platonic system would eliminate some dangers, about which the ancient Greeks were particularly sensitive, but they are convinced that the cure would be far more damaging than the social diseases supposedly eliminated by it. The average student, as he reads *The Republic,* feels nothing but pity for the children of the men and women who constitute the guardian class.

Though our ideology may have in it mixed and even contradictory elements, we are not ready to give up the family. The available evidence shows that more good life is likely to come by keeping the family than by any alternative which we can now imagine. Professor Nimkoff speaks for most of us when, in the Preface to his admirable book, *The Family,* he says, "Science has established two facts meaningful for human welfare: first, the foundation of the structure of human personality is laid down in early childhood; and second, the chief engineer in charge of this construction is the family."

Part of our present difficulty lies in the fact that we take the family unit so for granted that we fail to understand its meaning and its potential glory. We are normally almost as unconscious of it as we are of the air we breathe, but we begin to appreciate it when we have nearly lost it. Few spiritual tasks of our day are of more practical importance than a recovery of the wonder involved in the pattern of social structure which became the first major influence in most of our lives.

The family as we know it in the Western world is a composite of many factors, some Greek and some Roman, but the dominant factors are those which have come in the Judeo-Christian tradition. It is from this tradition that we have inherited the particular sort of sacredness which marriage involves and the particular sort of equality which obtains between family partners. Students, influenced more than they know by the dominant Biblical view of the family, are nearly always shocked by the passage at the end of the *Phaedo,* in which Socrates says explicitly that he did not wish to have his wife or other women with him during his last hours on earth. Such a passage would have been almost unthinkable after the Christian era had begun. The recovery of the Biblical pattern is nearly always beneficent and to this day the Jewish family life, when it is a conscious cultural inheritance, is probably the finest that our generation has to offer. By the beginning of the Christian era the Hebrew people had long rejected polygamy and had arrived at a settled conception of the family as existing primarily of two adults and their children, joined together in an intense fellowship, not merely for their own advantage but for the common good. This conception was passed on to the early Christians and through them to the whole of Western civilization.

How can we account for the sense of solemnity which nearly all persons feel when they observe a marriage ceremony? All feel that they are on holy ground because the dangers are so great and the opportunities so tremendous.

The gamble is for high stakes and it is for keeps! We do not feel a sense of awe about most human transactions; we do not feel like kneeling as we observe the deal of the automobile salesman; but we are filled with wonder when we watch two people, of opposite sex, as they stand before an altar and pledge their lifelong devotion to each other. Two people, who have never really lived together *at all*, undertake, by a sudden act, to live together all the rest of their lives. They thereby inaugurate something really novel in the world, their particular home, and their union is likely to result in the birth of new human beings, who would never have been born, in all eternity, apart from the particular decision which this ceremony expresses.

The joining of destinies has about it a really frightening quality. Henceforth sorrow for one will be sorrow for the other and good fortune for one will be good fortune for the other. If the husband is a failure in his work, the wife will share the consequent economic burden; if he commits a disgraceful public act, the wife shares the disgrace, and *vice versa*. It is of the essence of the undertaking, not only that each partner is thereby made the possible recipient of otherwise unknown joys, but that each, at the same time, is made highly *vulnerable*. The only way to make sure that one is never hurt is to refuse to make the gamble. It is the person who cares deeply, and has a stake in the enterprise, who can be most deeply wounded by the unfaithfulness of the partner.

Marriage always exacts a price, for both partners give up a great deal when they unite their two lives. The woman usually, though not always, gives up any further chance for academic training and worldly independence. She is likely to be handicapped, both physically and economically, by child bearing and by child care. Frequently she is so encumbered with small duties, that she feels that she has no opportunity to keep up her intellectual interests. She may come to the place where she greatly enjoys a community, only to be forced to leave it because her husband's vocational interests require that the family move to another place. At the same time the man gives up much. His marriage means that he is no longer free to use all that he earns for his own life and he can no longer give his entire attention to his profession, for a family necessitates the expenditure of time as well as of money. When the price is so high, is it not surprising that people continually pay it?

In one of her amusing but highly penetrating stories Dorothy Parker makes a young bride, at the beginning of her wedding trip, philosophize about the greatness of the leap which marriage represents and her sense of wonder that so many perform it. To the groom in the Pullman car she says, "When you think of all the people, all over the world, getting married just as if it was nothing. Chinese people and everybody. Just as if it wasn't anything." Her husband tries to get her mind off the universal aspect of the undertaking, but he does not succeed.

"I know," she said. "But I just sort of get to thinking of them, all over everywhere, doing it all the time. At least, I mean—getting married, you know. And it's—well, it's sort of such a big thing to do, it makes you feel queer. You think of them, all of them, all doing it just like it wasn't anything. And does, does anybody know what's going to happen next?"[4]

Out of all this excitement, aroused by the sense of possibility both for good and evil, there emerges the fair form of the family ideal, which continues to attract us, so that we make the leap and neglect the dangers. This ideal is something very precious, even though we illustrate it only in part and fitfully, and see it but dimly. We are concerned, at this point, not merely with modern man's unfortunate practice, but with the fairest dream we know. Our purpose must be to undergird it, to make it more explicitly understood and thereby to make it more likely to prevail. In this we get very little practical help from secular thought on the subject, but we get great help from specifically religious writings, such as the excellent contemporary volume, *Marriage and the Jewish Tradition,* by a group of able authors. For all our failures, the church, at this point at least, is still ahead of the world. What the historic faith, which stemmed originally from Palestine, has always maintained is that the meaning of marriage is not exhausted by its *biological, economic, psychological, legal* and *social aspects.* There is another aspect; it is *sacred.*

The sacredness of marriage as it has been developed in the Judeo-Christian pattern of human life is best understood by emphasis on three main features. *The first of these is the notion of commitment as against mere contract.* The point that marriage is more than a contract needs to be

[4] Dorothy Parker, *After Such Pleasures* (New York: The Viking Press, 1933). From the story "Here We Are."

given the widest possible dissemination, because many marriages owe their failure to a misunderstanding of this point. The first essential of marriage is the advance acceptance of the family relationship as *unconditional*. The father's responsibility to the child does not depend upon the child's health, his success or his character. The two participants in the marriage service pledge themselves, "for better and for worse." Frankly recognizing the dangers and pitfalls in advance, our religion tends to be intensely realistic rather than sentimental. The standardized service recognizes the strong possibility of economic difficulties, including real poverty, so the participants take each other "for richer, for poorer." One partner may become ill, one may be unable to become a parent, but this eventuality is recognized too; they take each other "in sickness and in health." Far from being a temporary affair, we pledge our troth "so long as we both shall live." If it were a contract it would have an escape clause.

It is this mood of commitment which distinguishes the family from worldly institutions and makes it intrinsically a religious institution. Commitment is the crucial step in religious experience. Faith, we know, when we think about it, is not merely intellectual assent to a set of propositions, but the supreme gamble in which we stake our lives upon a conviction. It is closer to courage than it is to mere belief. In this profound sense, marriage is an act of faith. Undoubtedly some dim understanding of this is very widespread, even in our highly secularized society, and this accounts for the fact that so many, who have no connection at all with any organized religion, turn to the church when marriage is planned. They sense, somehow, that the highest things belong together; they are sufficiently sensitive to realize that there is at least one human undertaking that is debased if it is wholly secularized. We may be a pagan generation, but it is highly revealing that we are not willing to take our paganism straight.

The commitment we call marriage is not a bargain! It is a situation in which each gives *all* that he has, including all his devotion and all of the fruits of his toil. "With *all* my worldly goods I thee endow." There is something extremely moving about the concept *all,* as everyone recognizes when he reads the gospel story of the widow's mite. This is part of the reason why almost every marriage ceremony is profoundly moving. The charming young woman gives *all* to this young man. The result is that marriage is an amazing relation in which the ordinary rules of business, with its contracts and escape clauses and limited liabilities, are despised and set aside. Marriage is no marriage at all if it is conditional or partial or with the fingers crossed. There must be, on both sides, an uncalculating abandon, a mutual outpouring of love and loyalty in a prodigal way. The best-loved story of the New Testament is a family story, the story not primarily of the prodigal son, but of the father who was prodigal in his affection, and the story of every truly married couple is the story of the prodigal pair. The enduring rule of marriage is "Love one another with all your mind and heart and body." The truly married person, finite though he be, is more interested in his mate's happiness than in his own, and his desire is to be to the other a constant delight. The fact that we do not achieve this ideal does not invalidate it.

The family is much older than our religion, and, as a natural grouping, would undoubtedly go on if our religion should come to an end, but the natural urges need a great deal of help and direction. The Judeo-Christian conception does not create the natural institution, but vastly improves it. It is like the Sabbath, in that it is a deliberate effort to facilitate holiness in the natural order. Marriage, as we have received it, is an attempt to produce a sanctuary out of a natural need. It is monogamy, but *monogamy plus*. It is the effort to make a holy path, not in separation from sex and work, or in seclusion, but in the midst of ordinary life. It thus maintains an ideal higher than that of the ascetic or monastic person. Marriage is the attempt to return man and woman to Paradise where they can live without sin. Such is our frailty, that this attempt does not wholly succeed, but the very effort is one of the noblest aspects of our common life. So long as marriage is seen as a holy commitment there is hope for our confused civilization.

The second main feature of marriage in the Judeo-Christian tradition is its public character. With one voice our best guides have told us that true marriage cannot be a private affair. Marriage is not primarily a device designed to provide personal pleasure to two people who pool their selfish interests. It is or can be a highly pleasurable undertaking, but the social responsibility involved is intrinsic. The union is likely to produce children who may be a burden or a strength to the outside community. It is therefore idle to tell the neighbors that it is none of their business. The family can never be a private institution because it contributes to the total good or ill of society; from it comes influence that affects mankind. The union of the parents of Abraham Lincoln affected millions besides themselves. In ancient Israel it was understood that the purposes of marriage were complex, rather than simple. It existed, they thought, to propagate the race, to satisfy emotional needs in beneficent ways and to perpetuate religious experience. In short, the family was understood as the fundamental unit of the social order.

The public significance of marriage has led to the formation of laws concerning both its establishment and its nullification. The common assumption of all such laws is that private or secret marriage is a contradiction in terms and quick marriage is always a failure to appreciate the total situation. The reason is that the community has a stake in the new union. A man and woman who begin living together with no further ado are outside the Judeo-Christian pattern because they are thereby denying the deep fact of community sharing. What we hold is that marriage, being intrinsically sacred, ought not to be consummated lightly, but should receive the blessing of a group who care. A wedding is a religious occasion during which a man and a woman make vows of lifelong fidelity, in the presence of those whose approbation they prize and whose blessing they seek.

The church is always insisting on the public nature of the marriage tie when it asks that the intention of marriage should be published "a proper time previous to the solemnization of it,"[5] and that the solemnization should not be experienced among strangers. At the Council of Trent much was made of the principle of *Proprius parochus*, the essence of this being the idea that, whenever possible, marriage is to be conducted in the parish of domicile. The purpose of the advice is that the judgment of local relatives, neighbors and clergy may thereby have more influence on the marriage. People care, and ought to care, about their reputations among those with whom they work and live. That is why divorce comes about so much more easily in an uprooted people. In the standard Quaker practice the couple intending marriage must seek the judgment of the local group to which they belong at least a month before the ceremony is performed. The Christian conscience has been consistently opposed to the existence of Gretna Greens, where runaway and secret marriages are made easy to the partners and profitable to the officials.

The third essential feature of marriage, in the Judeo-Christian tradition, is the free acceptance of a bond, something which limits the undisciplined self-expression which is natural to man. Just as marriage is not primarily for the personal pleasure of the couple concerned, likewise it is not compatible with absolute freedom. To the degree that full freedom of expression and action are primary to the code of modern man, our basic conception of marriage is endangered. The man who understands marriage is not thereby made blind to the physical attractiveness of women other than his wife, but the possibility of making love to

[5] *The Book of Church Order,* of the Presbyterian Church of the United States, Chap. XIII.

them is ruled out in advance. One big decision makes a host of minor decisions unnecessary. Free love, like private marriage, is a contradiction in terms, for conjugal love in many directions is real love in none.

Personal happiness must never become our chief end or goal. The purpose is not to be happy, but to perpetuate what is best for human life. Of course happiness usually comes in such a procedure, but it comes as a by-product. Emerson says wisely that the beauty of the sunrise or sunset is greatest when it comes as a surprise by the way. It is one lesson of the history of philosophical thought that the only way to *get* happiness is to *forget* it. Just as our popular philosophy is ambiguous about happiness it is likewise ambiguous about self-expression. Just what do we mean by it? *Which* side of ourselves do we propose to express? The idea of self-expression does not really help us, since the beastly side can be expressed just as the potential nobility can be expressed. Anyone who expressed all his thoughts and obeyed all his impulses would surely reveal himself as an utter fool.

The binding element is inherent in the family idea because without it, all the finer fruits of family love are impossible to produce. Marriage ties are permanently binding, not because a priest has said some words, but because an unbinding marriage is no marriage at all. The man who flits from one mate to another never really has *any*. But the central paradox is that the person who admits that he is bound thereby achieves the highest level of freedom; he is free from the superficiality of the philanderer. "Binding ties are welcome," says Felix Adler in a very profound sentence, "in so far as they are necessary to unbind what is highest in us."[6]

Against this Jewish background of the philosophy of freedom, Christian thought, beginning with the New Testament, has worked out a conception of freedom which elaborates the central paradox. Only those who have accepted some bondage are really free, we are told repeatedly. Freedom may be the moral goal, but it cannot be achieved directly; it must be earned. The mistake of so many in our generation is the fallacy of simplicity; they want freedom easily and cheaply, but they learn finally that it cannot be had in that market. What they get, instead, is a spurious article, which keeps them in permanent bondage to the passing appetites of the moment.

There is hardly any heresy more damaging to family life than the notion that we can live happily and well on a basis of inclination. All experience points in the opposite direction. G. K. Chesterton put the point with characteristic terseness when he wrote, "In everything on this earth that is worth doing, there is a stage when no one would do it except for necessity or honor."[7] The desire to escape family responsibilities is practically universal at some time or other and if mere inclination were followed every family would break to pieces. Separation on the ground of incompatibility is particularly inane, because all married couples are to some degree incompatible. "I have known many

[6] Stanley R. Brav, Ed., *Marriage and the Jewish Tradition*, (New York: Philosophical Library, 1952), p. 154.

[7] *Op. cit.*, p. 66.

happy marriages," says Chesterton, "but never a compatible one."[8]

Countless humble homes have been made scenes of enduring wonder by the fact that an *accepted bond* has held the members together in spite of hard work, poverty and much suffering. The visitor to the tiny Sandburg birthplace in Galesburg can hardly miss the sense of this wonder, especially when he reads the poet's own account of the constant struggle of the railroad blacksmith and his wife who lived in the tiny cottage.

Mama's wedding ring was never lost—was always on that finger as placed there with pledges years ago. It was a sign and seal of something that ran deep and held fast between the two of them. They had chosen each other as partners. How they happened to meet I heard only from my mother. . . . A smile spread over her face half bashful and a bright light came to her blue eyes as she said, "I saw it was my chance." She was saying this at least twenty years after the wedding and there had been hard work always, tough luck at times, seven children of whom two had died on the same day—and she had not one regret that she had jumped at her "chance" when she saw it.[9]

What, in the light of all this, are we to say about divorce? Some strands of our heritage accept divorce and some do not, but even those who reject divorce recognize the possibility of nullification. However high we raise our standard, we must take account of failure, and of marriages that are not real, whatever vows were once made. It will generally

[8] *Ibid.*, pp. 67, 68.
[9] Carl Sandburg, *Always the Young Strangers* (New York: Harcourt, Brace & Co., 1953), p. 8.

be agreed that this is not the kind of problem to be answered simply and legalistically by reference to some Biblical proof text. There is no doubt that Jesus sought to emphasize, as strongly as posssible, the enduring character of the marriage bond, but that is not to say we know what he would advise now if he were in the flesh in modern America. The question is complex and must be answered in the light of all of the human factors we can assemble.

In brief we may say that there are situations in which it is right to advise divorce not because divorce is good, but because the alternative is so bad. We have known couples who, after the recognition of early mistakes, have made new connections with high seriousness, and we could not but be glad. It would be a cruel judgment to say that their whole lives should be impoverished because of an initial mistake.

Having said this we must go on to say that all who care about the dignity of the family must resist easy divorce with all their power. Divorce must not be popular or admirable; it must always be an admission of failure in the most sacred undertaking of one's life. It may be the least of alternative evils, but it certainly is not a positive good. Above all we must maintain that the exception does not become the rule. It is still of the essence of marriage that it should be binding, even though in some instances the bond is broken.

The willing acceptance of a bond needs to be stressed more thoroughly in regard to marriage than in most human associations, because what we are trying to keep is of higher value. It is roughly true to say that the effort required is directly proportional to the value of what is being maintained and nurtured. Matter endures easily; life is more precarious in its existence than matter is; and spiritual experience is more precarious still. The sacredness of the family is hard to maintain, because the ideal is so high; like any fine instrument, it can be ruined with relative ease.

The family is the custodian and only true example of life's highest known ideal. It is the one institution in which it is possible to say "we" without any loss of individuality. It is each for all and all for each, as is never the case in a secular society and seldom in a religious society. To say "we" and to mean it, is a very great spiritual achievement for the nominative plural is the noblest of the personal pronouns. A family in which each does what he can and each receives what he needs, wholly without financial calculation of earning or merit, represents the highest known ideal, our only true approximation to the Kingdom of God, yet countless humble families, made up of fallible persons, demonstrate this ideal in great measure every day of their lives. This is a foretaste of what the world ought to become. The categorical imperative for every family is this: So act that the fellowship of the family becomes an advance demonstration of the heavenly kingdom.

Because this is a book about the family and not specifically about marriage, there is no need for us to engage in any extended discussion of sexual experience except as this bears on the production of children who augment the family circle. Suffice it to say that the physical union of the sexes, which marriage glorifies, has two main purposes. One purpose is the production of new persons and the other purpose is the expression of deep affection. One of the most significant things to say about sexual intercourse is that it provides husband and wife with a *language* which cannot be matched by words or by any other act whatsoever. Love needs language for its adequate expression and sex has its own syntax. Since sexual intercourse for the second purpose is and ought to be far more frequent than for the first purpose, any serious discussion of the life of the family must face the problem of the deliberate limitation of the size of the family which is popularly known as birth control or planned parenthood.

Though there are important differences on the point of method, nearly all who think about the matter favor some kind of birth control. Some advocate birth control by celibacy, some by the complete cessation of sexual experience except when children are desired, some by the recognition of "safe times" in a rhythm of natural fertility and sterility, some by the use of practical devices which modern technology and medicine have made possible. There are, of course, times for continence, and no genuine marriage is possible without restraint, particularly for the man, but most who think about it advocate use of some method which does not involve continuous abstinence. The reason is that the limitation of sexual experience to the few times when there is an effort to produce children seems a crude and foolish impoverishment of human life.

There are, of course, dangers involved in any civilization in which devices for birth control are easy of access, especially for the young, but we may as well understand that we shall not turn the clock back in this regard. The way of wisdom here, as in relation to all products of our mechanical age, is to learn to use such things as the means to the good life and not its destruction. The test lies not in the invention, but in its human use. From the strictly moral point of view the case for some kind of birth control is very strong indeed. The chief moral considerations are that unrestricted childbearing is harmful to parents, especially to the mother who may become terribly depleted and overworked, and that it is harmful to the children if so many are born that adequate opportunities are open to none. That such considerations now seem persuasive to nearly all parts of our civilization, including a great variety religiously and racially, is evident from the contrast between the size of the ordinary family in our day and in our grandparents' day. When our daughter was born, she was the one hundred sixty-sixth descendant of a living woman, her great-grandmother Marshall. The chance that we or any of our contemporaries shall match Mrs. Marshall is very slight.

Already the fad of the small family is over, and for this we can be thankful. Planned parenthood did not bring the childless home, as some feared, and we have reason to believe that something of a reasonable balance has already been achieved. One beneficent feature has been a vast increase in the number of early marriages, partly because of the war which hastened an ideological change. On the whole this change has been wholesome and the practice of earlier beginning of family life may be expected to continue.

Another hopeful sign is the great change that has occurred in general philosophy in regard to the adoption of children. Once, in the memory of many living persons, adoption was carried on in an atmosphere of secrecy and almost of shame. Many adopted children did not learn, until they were adults, that they had been adopted, with the result that the revelation of the secret was sometimes psychologically catastrophic. Now the practice of adoption is admired and widely publicized, while the children in the transaction are told at the earliest possible moment that they are able to understand. The consequence is that the average adopted child is hugely pleased that he was *chosen* and not taken on as a forced gift. Now adoption is so acceptable that there are not enough available children to meet the mounting demand. If changes as big as these can come in a short time, others can come also, and they will come if we understand sufficiently what the family *means*, both to its members and to society at large.

In concluding this chapter it may be necessary to say that marriage has no magic about it. The family can be the scene of wonderful affection and it can also be the scene of debasing friction. The family, as depicted in the foregoing pages, is our fairest human ideal, but it does not come without effort. Family solidarity takes hard work, much imagination and constant self-criticism on the part of all the members of the sacred circle. A successful marriage is not one in which two people, beautifully matched, find each other and get along happily ever after because of this initial matching. It is, instead, a system by means of which persons who are sinful and contentious are so caught by a dream bigger than themselves that they work throughout the years, in spite of repeated disappointment, to make the dream come true.

CHAPTER III

The Vocation of Married Women

> The great majority of women go out into the world
> to a single occupation. . . . Because that single occupa-
> tion has not been regarded as an intellectual occupa-
> tion, I venture to think that this is one of the greatest
> mistakes civilized men and women have committed.
>
> CHARLES W. ELIOT

MARRIAGE is a career for a woman as it can never be
for a man. It is not sufficient to say that there are
mothers and fathers and to equate their contributions.
The family is a group of people, but as individuals they
do not contribute equally to the family life. A man, a
woman and children make the unit, but the woman is at
the center, and the lives of the others are good in the
degree to which the woman takes her calling seriously,
making their welfare her major concern.

The romance of marriage, combining as it does the
highest emotional experience of human life with the great
adventure of a new career, makes a sane consideration of
marriage almost impossible for young women. A career
which is not mixed up with human love would be much
more easily discussed. Every woman who has conformed

to the conventional pattern by devoting her life with single mind to the family, of which she is the center, has something relevant to say on the subject, yet how to say it is not easy. Young women must be very curious about the thoughts that go on inside the heads of mature women. Therefore this chapter will be in the first person, quite different from the other chapters of this book.

More than ever before, our century has seen great changes in the lives of women, changes which have forced them to consider the wide variety of categories in which the twentieth century has placed them. Men have changed more slowly through the ages and have not been forced to consider their station to the same degree. Therefore they continue to think of women's lives in the way in which they desire them, until firsthand experience awakens them rudely. They think in terms of their personal relationships to wives, mothers, daughters, sisters, while in the outside world they think of women as employable, in many phases of men's work. Women find that they are faced with a situation much more complex than the men understand it to be, one group having even less in common with another than stenographers have with shipbuilders because women are separated from other women by their views of life more than by kinds of work.

Today we have to think in terms of single women with private incomes who live in their own homes without making much contribution to society, of single women who have careers or professions comparable to those of men or the same as those of men, of single women who work for men sympathetically and helpfully, of single women as day laborers, of married women who are contented home-makers, of married women who are frustrated home-makers, of married women with careers and professions, of married women as industrial and as clerical workers, of married women as part-time earners (some necessarily so and others by choice), of widows who live on the estates of their husbands, of widows who contribute time and money to humanitarian causes, of widows who earn a partial living, of widows who must have a career or profession to support children, of widows in industry or common labor who support children, even of divorcees—all this is too complex to contemplate. In whatever manner it may be necessary for a woman to live her life, the problems are worthy of attention. This chapter, however, must be confined to the role of those women who are trying to solve the problems of family life as the twentieth century has created them. If other chapters are needed, may qualified women have the courage to produce them.

Of course, it is a paradox to think in terms of what married women have to say because, for the most part, they have been silent. I recognize the difficulty I am in. The relationship of a happily married couple is a highly emotional one since a relationship without emotion is not marriage, but there is no surety in how it will be expressed. It is like art in that there will be more of the sordid variety than of the truly great. Women, recognizing the emotional nature of their calling, fear that they will reveal more than they intend. Emotion, however, has occasionally sent women seeking paper and ink as an expression. One must care in order to write; a motivation is necessary or the writing fails to come off. Mrs. Carlyle wrote when she was angry with Thomas, Mrs. Browning in the flush of love, Mrs. Trollope wrote from need and a loquacious tendency which is often called gossip or curiosity about one's fellows, Mrs. Woolf, in a room of her own, maintained her intellectual integrity and literary skill, demonstrating thereby an especially sophisticated form of feminism.

Novels have been a most popular form of feminine writing. Those using the indirect form have not offended by seeming to know too much too surely. Women today often become professional writers by writing like men (or, at least, not differently from men) on the subjects which interest men and, until recently, under masculine names. Publishers find it fairly easy to use such articles, but the moment a woman begins to write her own ideas about the relationship of men and women there is an emotional reaction on the part of men and women alike. Few women have had the ability to write objectively on this subject. It would be much easier to write this chapter if I could choose my readers. Words can be color words for men when women relish them. In like manner, angels would fear to tread between the groups of women. Because men like to think that women should be angels they feel that a married woman is out of character if she presumes to tell the world what she thinks. And men are right, because often she *is* out of character. Wives and mothers cherish and love, and speaking one's mind is almost certain to hurt the feelings of some innocent bystander.

The strain between the generations of married women

today is very largely based on contrasting conceptions of the danger of wounding the feelings of other people. The great majority of women over sixty are inhibited. Even though they are well educated many of them will not risk differing in opinion with the spoken word in public, though they are not always so reserved in private company. Women in middle age are usually willing to express their thinking, but they recognize that many of the older women will think them most unladylike. Young women in increasing numbers not only feel free, but many of them are as well trained as the young men to think objectively and to express their views in public gatherings and in the press. The older women remember the emancipation of women and they fear the emotional forces which are inherent in that emancipation. The young women, however, have no understanding of these forces. Taught to share public life and community life on a basis of equality until married, it is not surprising that young women expect to continue the same participation after marriage. Education leads them to expect this halcyon state of affairs.

While the women who receive a college education constitute only a minority, as is likewise true of men, these minorities nevertheless set the patterns for life for all in a large measure. The young women are unaware that husbands in middle life will expect them to be contented wives, finding adequate expression in homemaking. The contentment of the happily married woman, which the men presuppose, is not likely to produce writing, for writing comes out of tension or concern. Contentment produces good living with emotional overtones.

Granted, then, that I am writing out of character, I must try to say how it is possible. In a sense my generation are hybrids. Many of us have achieved contentment, but only through tension resolved. Since my concern for our family has been my major interest for twenty-nine years, I have found it necessary to find an intellectual interpretation of that concern which would give me a sense of integration while I did it. I had to know why I was willing to give up the opportunity of doing a number of other things to which I felt drawn (particularly architecture, which was an inherited aptitude) in order to do this one thing which marriage required of me. I belong to that first generation of women who could have both a career and marriage without losing social status. In fact the American Association of University Women assured any girl social status by virtue of graduation. But those of us who have played the role of wife in the twentieth century have seen this supposed benefit deteriorate. Modern ideas of what education does for a woman have sometimes been peculiarly inadequate when a particular woman has had to work out her relationship to a particular man.

However many women continue to function in the natural role of wife, the minority who get divorces is increasing. One divorce out of four marriages is alarming! Young men in our colleges today are positively frightened about what marriage may bring to them. It is not only disturbing to young men, it is equally disturbing to parents of sons. A woman may be shortsighted enough to deplore too much independence and male ego in her husband, but she hopes that some young woman will help her son to maintain these masculine qualities as he works with other men in our highly competitive society.

The work of married women is not all active; much of it is necessarily passive. Sometimes a wife and mother is doing her work best when she is seemingly doing nothing. Though I know that most of the things older women say are of no avail, I write somewhat in the hope that I can help stem the tide of divorce by interpreting what it is that a woman is doing while she seems to do nothing. Women older than I am think these things cannot be said, but must be learned by experience. But the point is that the person with experience *can* say it. Alcoholism cannot be stopped by merely saying it is evil and harmful; it takes the understanding of Alcoholics Anonymous to save the alcoholics. The physician and surgeon does not wait for the young medical student to learn by experience alone. Dr. Osler is the great example, the perfect combination of inspiration and teaching, in order to make experience lead in the right direction. Because of the high incidence of failure in family life, women must try to emulate Dr. Osler.

Men and women have the God-given privilege of complementing one another. Any individual life is meagre by comparison with all the variety of ways in which human lives have flowered through the ages. Marriage insures that each one will live more fully because of the contribution of the other. Marriage stretches the powers of men and women, their understanding and their wisdom. The Jewish religion and the Christian faith have made the marriage relation a means of expressing the relation of man to God. As the Christian must lose his soul to save it, so the greatest love between a man and woman is that in which a wife so trusts her husband that she has no fear in promising to obey him. The Christian discipline for wives is found in Titus 2:3-5 (R.S.V.):

Bid the older women likewise to be reverent in behaviour,... they are to teach what is good, and so train the young women to love their husbands and children, to be sensible, chaste, domestic, kind, and submissive to their husbands, that the word of God may not be discredited.

This is not a counsel for the wives of pagan men. Wives of Christian men will find the submissive role full of rewards.

The feminist movement was born of atheist parentage. Self-centered women were concerned for their right to live as men live. Wives of men who were not Christian in their practice were easy prey to the arguments of women who sought equal rights by law. Christian people defended the right of women to be treated justly and the feminists, who cared nothing for the feminine virtues, won the legal right to be equal competitors of men. Equality through complement is the Christian relationship of men and women, but the ardent feminist was not concerned with this relationship. The Christian single woman likewise ought not to be concerned with competition with men, for competition is not a Christian virtue. The feminine single woman who contributes to a man the same understanding of his work in the world as a wife does to his personal life becomes the indispensable secretary, the peaceful personnel worker, the orderly executive of a department. The right relationship to men in working for them and with them requires insight of a high order.

We are concerned here with the woman who has loved and been loved by a man in the legal status of marriage. Such women were among those who received the first education shared by men and women on equal terms. It has been my good fortune to know a number of this tiny minority of women. Usually their education stressed liberal arts as the basis of the curriculum. I observed that the education they received had not prevented them from being contented wives and mothers. They were keenly intellectual, but they had married in the normal fashion and had become homemakers. I tried, as a young wife, to discover the secret of their contentment. They intrigued me and I wanted to know how they resolved the tension of intellectual interest and domesticity. I watched them for the answers not found in words. Husbands of such women, some of whom were distinguished men, sometimes gave me a clue. I found I could learn by acquaintance.

Literature is a mirror of men's minds. I began a search for the answers to women's relationship to men. Through the years I have found a few marvelous examples of conscious interpretation on the part of married women. Some of these writings, most relevant to the vocation of married women, have never been published. I have read them in manuscript, hidden in library vaults though they were. Two such books have been privately printed for the members of the family only. These women writers have proved to me that it is possible for married women to write of their relationship to husband and children without emotion or sentimental self-interest. While men may consider that it is out of character for a woman to write directly and with a measure of objectivity about her vocation, it may be that women will not have the same opinion. At least it has seemed to me that these women whose journals I have read were writing very much in character, and most helpfully to meet my need. To interpret one's deepest convictions is surely a better teaching technique than to solve the problems of others in detail. This leaves self-respect, a commodity much prized by human beings.

Writing, then, is a medium of sharing which has not been much used by women in the direct form. Even those who have indulged in it have not often sought publication. A well-known professor of English in our time once said that "any woman who gave birth to a baby at the North Pole could write an article about it and have it accepted by the best literary magazines, but a scholar in a field of English would have a very poor chance of getting an article published." A woman would find it equally difficult in a scholarly field. *The Egg and I* found a publisher because a woman's ire is in character and can be appreciated by men, particularly if it is expressed humorously. But when a woman writes as a loving wife she is likely to sound banal. Virginia Woolf complained that publishers would not publish that which she wished to have published. There is a sense in which men and professional women are unable to see the market for articles women wish to write and read. The women's magazines were the best hope until career women came on the scene. "Fifty Years Ago" in *The Ladies' Home Journal* will surely lose its humorous touch when the nineteen-forties are the source material (unless careers for women have become humorous by that time.)

The conventional married woman is still among us and remains in the majority, but she is inarticulate. Men continue to love her partly because men prefer her inarticulate. She is often the woman who has used her intelligence in producing good family life, establishing normal routine with a rhythm that allows the introduction of variety. Some such women are experts, but there is no yardstick by which to measure their achievement, no recognition by which to honor the stages on the way to success. Women need to share with one another their ways of finding contentment in their work. Either men must encourage the contented woman to speak or learn to speak satisfactorily in her behalf or they will lose her. When woman has been taught to speak she must be allowed to speak. The Quaker women have been allowed to speak in religious meetings of the Society of Friends, as equals before God, for over three hundred years, but feminism has never won that right for the women of the churches.

Hal Boyle, in one of his syndicated colums, says,

The greatest woman in history is—the American housewife. But too often she has an inferiority complex. At cocktail parties, particularly if there are career women present, she is likely to murmer when introduced, "Oh, I'm nobody. I don't do anything. I'm just a housewife." Actually, of course, she is proud of being a housewife. But she feels that nobody else thinks her job is either important or thrilling.

Too often she is right. I don't say myself that the shop talk of wives is always as interesting as the reminiscences of actresses or lady wrestlers. But few professional career women live a life one-half as exciting or satisfying as that of the ordinary housewife. Motherhood, the art of raising children, is an endless drama, a ceaseless adventure.

It is better for me to quote these words of Hal Boyle, with the prestige of his syndicated column, than to use my own, because I am "just a housewife," but the rest of his article will not accomplish all that he hopes it will, though as a married woman I am very grateful to him for his generous words. The masculine slant at one or two points, however, is more damaging to his case than he realizes. When he says, "I don't say myself that the shop talk of wives is always as interesting as the reminiscences of actresses or lady wrestlers," he has undone much that he hoped to achieve in his article. Women want to be interesting enough to be in on the conversation as equals. Of course the shop talk of baseball league players or of washing machine salesmen might not be interesting to Hal Boyle either. Shop talk, whatever the subject, should be confined to those of like profession, men as well as women.

When Mr. Boyle says, "Actually, of course, she is proud of being a housewife," he is saying what every man hopes is the truth. Women know better. Only a few women are proud of being housewives today. The great majority of women do not get pride out of their job as housewives. Pride goes with a sense of achievement and because women have no way of measuring their success or of winning recognition for ability, not even in so mundane a way as monetary return, they are usually unable to enjoy a sense of success. Modern women, knowing from experience the satisfaction of working where standards and goals give a chance for recognition for outstanding ability, find it very hard to adjust to a role where short-time gains are not obvious.

Women who have identified their lives with the public lives of men find it possible to enter into the social conversation of men. After marriage a woman soon finds that she has lost this entree. A married woman finds her social life one of segregation; the men in one corner, the women in the other. There is no use to rebel, this is the way the men want it. They like a masculine group because they have a special regard for feminine women, and masculine talk must always be limited in the presence of ladies. The women may be willing to forego being ladies for the sake of free conversation, but ladies bring up the kind of men who value ladies.

Now when Mr. Boyle says that "few professional career women live a life one-half as exciting or satisfying as that of the ordinary housewife" he is not fair in comparing the work of a married woman with the career of a professional woman, because the two are not in the least comparable. The exciting part of a married woman's life is in the love life which marriage makes sinless. The women are proud to be chosen as sweethearts and potential mothers, rather than for the great profession of housewife. (Housekeeping is the chosen career of some women.) Whether the women choose the career of housewife or not it is what they get if they choose the "exciting role of wife" or the "ceaseless adventure" of motherhood.

Of course the men have always taken the housewife for granted. They know her role is one that really matters and they hope above hope that the women they marry will love to be housewives. A contented housewife is a prize above rubies these days, but the men are unable to make the women satisfied with this role, at least in most cases. Either the women are going to have to deal with this problem, or the men are going to have to change their ways. Since I am a woman I must apply myself to the first of these alternatives.

The Constitution of our country was an experiment in government and it continues to be the proving ground for much else besides. Experiments continue to go on and, through our laws, we have been able to work the greatest experiment in the education of women that the world has known. There is something in the spiritual basis of our country that makes it inevitable that women should have freedom. If they choose freedom from homemaking there is little the government can do to prevent them.

Perhaps this great experiment in educating women like men has now continued long enough for us to evaluate it. If we are to evaluate it we must know how it arose. There is a gap in knowledge which affects all of us more or less, but in our time the ill effects of a gap are probably more damaging than ever before. When the generations live near each other and when the tempo of life is slower there is the opportunity to fill in this gap with conversation, since every family has some members with the gift of relating family and community lore. This was a form of entertainment in former times, a way of bridging the gap between history and literature as taught, and the present. When our two older boys were small they loved to stretch out on their stomachs on the floor and read *Who's Who in America.* It seemed a strange pastime for small boys. It was a way in which they came to know what had been going forward while they were growing up and which could not get into their textbooks. Every intelligent college student deplores the fact that he has no time to read current literature.

In a time of great change the recent past holds the key to our right understanding of our relationship to life. I belong to a generation of women born into a new period of history which we took for granted, but which we neither understood nor feared. The emancipation of women was a *fait accompli* and we took education and the right to vote as our natural rights. Women older than I am have very different feelings, for emotion enters into their thinking about education and the franchise. Contemporary men of this older generation think of these rights with emotion also, some in defense, some in disdain. But my generation of women and our contemporaries, the men, understand very little about the feminist movement, unless we have made a private study of it, and the gap in our knowledge has caused a great deal of frustration in the lives of married women. The freedom to live like men was ours for the choice, but the great majority chose marriage and then found that much was required which they had not expected. For the first time in history married women saw their single sisters enjoying the freedom to fulfill their ambition in the work of their choice, while those who married kept house, had babies, and made the money stretch in the time-honored fashion which uneducated women had seemed to do equally well, in some cases, in former generations. No one had taken the trouble to tell the married women how their education applied.

Education leads men and women to think they can choose their work up to the level of their ability. This has had significance for the men and for a few women, but for the majority of women it is irrelevant. "The single woman may choose any profession she pleases, but a married woman has her profession cut out for her."[1] Marriage for women means the career of homemaking. Men expect it to mean that to a woman all the while that they are teaching them to think precisely, to be efficient in their laboratory techniques, to meet the state requirements for the teaching profession, etc., and they do not take into account that they are *untraining* them for the role of wife. Men cannot hold the two areas of life, public and private, in the lives of women, in the same context. Some women they indoctrinate in the working world of men. That these women may become wives and mothers, unfitted for their role, is no concern of the men who teach them or train them in special ways for business or industry. The fallacy of these men is that they assume that women are endowed by nature to fit into the pattern of family life as it has been adapted to the twentieth century. Educators know that human beings are molded, directed, motivated by educa-

[1] Felix Adler in *Marriage and the Jewish Tradition*, p. 157.

tional processes, yet they naïvely expect that women will revert to the time-honored responses to the basic human need for family life. Fortunately it is impossible to divert some women in the first place.

To the traveler in the United States it is noticeable that the women of the south have not lost their sense of pride in the feminine role of homemaking. The traditions of the south are derived from a way of life in which men prize and encourage the feminine virtues. The gallant courtesy of many men sets a pattern by which women are enabled to understand their own function. For this reason education in the south is on the whole more successful in preserving the dignity of the domestic life. They have not forgotten that gracious living is dependent on the relaxation and contentment of many people, but particularly of women in homes.

The terrible possibilities of manipulating men's minds is now obvious to all. With the great examples of Nazism and Communism, with the evidence of how children can be taught a vicious political gospel that will turn them against their own parents, and the ways in which ideas can dominate a human being until he loses his personality or his mental powers, even uneducated people know something of the degree to which ideas have consequences. Women cannot be educated and taught to work like men and then experience no frustration in living like women. It is the universality of a woman's contribution which she must understand. "The peculiar gift of woman, it seems to me, is to see life as a whole—hers is, as it were, the assembling function; the peculiar gift of man is specialization; the exercise of energy along specific lines."[2]

Men are in a dilemma. They did not ask to have women educated like men. It was foisted upon them by a crusading minority of aggressive women, aided and abetted by married feminine women who believed in justice for all, including themselves if they should ever need it. Men have accepted the women into their area of public life and have educated them for it with reluctance and, at times, with dragging feet. They have not attempted to teach women those things which they do not know how to teach. Christian women have asked only that they be treated as equals if dire necessity should place them in the position of needing to earn a living. Feminists want to work to prove not only equality, but superiority if possible. More recently women want to work because they are not satisfied with being "merely" wives and mothers. A great many disdain the feminine area of employment. Chesterton says in *What's Wrong with the World*, "Most of the Feminists would probably agree with me that womanhood is under shameful tyranny in the shops and mills. But I want to destroy the tyranny. They want to destroy the womanhood."[3] Chesterton wrote this in 1901, but more than fifty years later the truth of what he says is only too obvious.

Men need feminine women who are willing to use their minds to make family life good and complement their lives. However, women who would enjoy this career are often

[2] Adler, *ibid.*, p. 161.
[3] Pp. 224, 225.

victims of a slogan used by the feminists when they were campaigning for equal education for women. This slogan was designed to strike fear in the hearts of married women so that they, too, would favor masculine education for women. This slogan was, "What would you do if your husband should die?" Even today some young women are getting an education in order to be prepared for tragedy. There are too many feminists yet living for the slogan to die, but it has been superseded.

The practical problem before a married woman is that her efforts to be useful in the world are often resented by the people of both sexes who have vested professional interests. How can able women share their ideas and use their increasing leisure to perform needed tasks without antagonizing those who think of these tasks as their own particular spheres of professional competence? The danger is that the answers will be given too lightly. The politician will say, "Very good, come along, you can count the ballots on election day." The college president will ask, "Would you manage the teas for the winter musical programs?" The public school administrator will say, "Fine, join the P.T.A. and see what fine programs we put on." Women are welcome in public life if they will fit in without making a difference.

Often, when projects are planned, the promoters, who think of themselves as experts, envisage a situation in which the lay people give financial support in order that the experts may have the satisfaction of manipulating the lives of these same lay people. There is something faintly insulting about the ordinary use of the term layman, in the mouths of experts, and lay men must often feel it, but it is women who have occasion to feel it nearly all the time. The highly trained expert asks, "How can we get them to finance our projects without taking their ideas?"

If it is right that married women must always be lay persons in public life then we should make their domestic life of such importance that we educate them for it. One of the chief reasons why such professions as law and medicine carry with them an inherent sense of dignity is that everyone knows that they require specialized education for their successful practice. Since women cannot receive a professional training for their lifework, they think they must be trained for another profession in order to be accepted as worthy of attention. Herein lies our basic confusion. It is wasteful to train women for professions in which they will never engage or at most will spend only a few interim years. An education planned realistically for the mature woman as she will use it after marriage seems like a reasonable suggestion. The earned degree is irrelevant to a married woman's life, but education, which is a different matter, is of paramount importance.

Every opportunity for education is open to women today, but work which does not require a college degree is often better paid and social status is no longer an issue. Since widows are not novices the requirements placed on inexperienced people ought not to apply to them. They are highly experienced persons, able to adapt and adjust and to carry heavy responsibilities. In these days they are likely to be better educated and have higher I.Q.'s than the people who hold the positions for which they compete.

If men would make a more flexible situation in the requirements for widows who need to support children they would be doing a very important thing, in that they would take the fear out of the hearts of married women including their own wives and daughters. What do men want most, competition at every point or contented wives at home?

The teaching profession is a case in point. Mothers have experience in teaching children which ought to be recognized. Formerly teachers were highly respected because they were people with mental ability and often from the most cultivated families. Now we have a system calculated to train people with average intelligence to educate children some of whom have more native intelligence than their teachers. Many superior people are teachers who need professional protection, but the existent teachers cannot cope with the large numbers of children in our schools today. The young women who have intelligence and personality would be serving society better if they used the two or three years that they have before marriage in teaching children, under the direction of professional teachers, than in spending so much of their college life in such a specialized field as education. The young women know this, but faculties have not faced the fact that most of the women are taking their education in a most Pickwickian sense.

Mothers often find that the teachers of their children are not so intellectually able and often not as highly educated as themselves, but our laws and conventions were not made for such a time as this. The existence of educated women in large numbers means that women in homes are no longer "just housewives" though the professional people still insult them at every turn. To be talked down to because one has no tag to her name to indicate her degree of intellectual ability, because she belongs to the masses called Mrs., is the lot of many a young mother. We are wasting our woman power by the outrageous notion that teachers with mere training are better than natural teachers. If allowed to do so, many women with ability would be glad to teach for limited periods thus lifting the load from the overworked professional teachers. We are grateful for the excellent teachers in our public schools, but there are not enough of them and our children are not always fortunate.

It has been my privilege to converse with many wives in my travels with my husband. I am always on the fringes of every public occasion which we attend, meeting the other women who are also on the fringes. We all know what it is to have our husbands introduced, with the opportunity of making a reply, while we are introduced in a manner which assumes that we are unable to make any response at all. We rise and smile. Personally, I should rather be ignored. If I could say even a few words I should feel more like a human being. This convention must be a hangover from the days when women were unprepared to speak in public, so that they were easily put into a flutter and it was more gallant not to expect anything from them. Surely there is no woman today who cannot meet such a requirement if she has the position in which the occasion will occur.

A young woman once told me that she was having a very hard time to adjust to her married role because she had been a practicing social worker before her marriage and now people came to their home to discuss social problems with her husband, a trained religious worker, but paid no attention to anything she said. Recently, in England, I heard a wife who had married late, after years of experience in social work, say that she was unprepared for the sudden loss of station that had come to her with marriage. The lack of expectancy on the part of people who assume that married women will not have valuable judgments is at the heart of the unrest in educated women's lives.

The greatest gift any woman could give to womankind in this twentieth century would be a new word, to signify her relationship to life if she marries. No single word now in use does this. We need a new word, which, defined, means a companion creating a home, a center of civilization which can save the world if there are enough of them. We need a word which signifies that a mother is a person of wisdom and insight, devoting her intellectual ability to the task of turning children into mature, Christian people. This is a most difficult profession and, while we do not get meritorious awards for achievement, we do get all the pain and sense of shame that goes with failure. If Hitler's mother had been gifted in her profession there would never have been a Hitler as the world knows him. We need a word which signifies the achievement possible to woman, a word indicating her hopes about her station, which the world will use the way we use other words signifying competence. Mother covers the physical act of bearing and rearing children, wife means legal sweetheart, warning away all others, homemaker means a person who organizes a place for the benefit of a family and gives her major thought to it, housewife means a person who does the physical work of maintaining a house and the services to the individuals in it. We need a word which joins all of these and, in addition, means creator of spiritual values, teacher of the young, developer of human abilities and harmonizer of personalities as well. A new word, said with the respect which we employ in reference to physician, minister or statesman, might be more important than volumes of discussion.

Naturally any new word sounds awkward at first, even if it comes from the most respectable classic roots, but, if it really meets a need, it finally sounds right. One possible name for the person who has dedicated herself to the vocation described in this chapter is *agathelian*, an adaptation of θηλεα, a word with highly feminine connotations.[4] Here we have a close approximation to the old term "good wife" but in form comparable to that used to denote members of learned professions. Those who are tired of saying they are "just housewives" may wish to cause consternation by answering that they are agathelians.

Marriage for women is, perhaps, not so much a profession, however, as a ministry. A ministry is a service and the work of married women is service of several orders. The fact that there is no monetary compensation and that the hours are indefinite puts a woman's work in the class of service. I prefer the word ministry myself, because I hon-

[4] This word has been coined in co-operation with Dr. William E. Berry, beloved professor of Greek, and Mrs. Berry. We hope it is at least amusing.

estly do not think a woman can succeed in her vocation without the same kind of commitment which we give to the Christian Cause when we become active Christians.

The place of married women in society needs to be defined, not so much in terms of what women want as in terms of what their station requires of them. It has occurred to me that great illumination can come by a consideration of the station of a soldier and his duties. War is a great evil, but it may provide the lesson that some women need to make them satisfied with marriage as a career. For the wife as for the soldier, discipline is required, and it is a good thing for women to know that their calling is not the only one requiring sacrifice of personal freedom. The incidence of death is sobering as the great moment for the drama of war or birth takes place. Modern warfare is not so costly in human life as in the past and modern medical research now saves the lives of many mothers who would have been victims in former years. For some men a military career is the choice for life; some women find complete fulfillment in keeping house. The majority of men would rather choose other careers, but war prevents them; women are prevented by marriage. When compulsory military service drafts men some achieve competence in a particular service which brings them satisfaction, even though it is not a first choice. This is the experience of many women who adapt themselves happily to work which they would not have chosen. The experience of enlistment cannot easily be avoided and love has a compelling power to require a woman to accept those duties which marriage imposes. A few women find ways of escape after marriage

and after motherhood which we might be willing to con-
done, but the great majority are committed to the joint
enterprise so fully that success can only come by complete
submission. War makes a soldier's life one of uncertainty.
He goes where duty calls; he may have service which is
utter boredom. In similar fashion many educated women
find the life of a homemaker full of service which is utter
boredom to them. Neither the soldier nor the wife can
change station with honor. The one-fourth of married
women today who get divorces probably have a large per-
centage among them who are simply unwilling to accept
the necessary discipline for motherhood. Many more who
are not divorced are equally undisciplined.

Part of the discipline may be the willingness to forego
much of public life. I am not sure that it is possible for
married women to live true to their vocation as wives and
mothers and participate in community life on a basis of
equality. This observation will not make experienced
wives happy, even though it is their confirmed opinion; it
will not even be believed by young women who, having experienced equality, think the world has progressed to a
new relationship in marriage. A generation of women who
once thought the same have come to doubt the reality of
the vision, now or ever. The current thought is that the
men must be taught to accept the idea of equal sharing of
home life and work in the world, a fifty-fifty basis being
considered fair. Though marriage courses in the colleges
have exploited this latest solution to the problem of
freedom for women, it only postpones the evil day when
truth must be faced. The great majority of women will

continue to live in a world of their own and the great majority of men will continue to control public institutions until the Kingdom of God comes on earth.

Motherhood is a profession which rests in part on the technical knowledge required for housekeeping. A Japanese mother once told me that her first six children were girls and at that period in her life she took them regularly to Sunday School and church. They were always there in freshly laundered dresses looking their best. When asked how she achieved this high standard of performance she said, "I always began on Thursday." Their spiritual life was so important to her that she began on Thursday to make her housekeeping the background for it.

Housework must have been designed by God to keep a woman busy so that she would be at home, but too occupied to control the lives of the members of her family overmuch. Neither is she a servant. No, she is just there, often in the background, quite busy, always feeling the environment and the changes and chances that make every person in the house respond and react. She is gathering data which in some future situation may prove to be invaluable. Mothers need to know what is happening to the minds and souls of their children. Since they can never know enough, the woman who is always available has the greatest opportunity. As children mature mothers draw on the whole past to guide them as they withdraw discipline and substitute the fellowship of equality of mature people. Mothers are able to discern the secret sorrows and the secret hopes of their children because they have disciplined themselves in order to know their children as only a person who forgets herself can know them. Chesterton says it succinctly:

> Babies need not to be taught a trade, but to be introduced to a world. To put the matter shortly, woman is generally shut up in a house with a human being at the time when he asks all the questions that there are, and some that there aren't. Now if anyone said that this duty of general enlightenment is in itself too exacting and oppressive, I can understand the view. I can only answer that our race has thought it worthwhile to cast this burden on women in order to keep common sense in the world.[5]

We find, then, not one ministry for married women, but three. There are other strands of a woman's life which exist for all, but in marriage three ministries may be performed by women even when they are not mothers: the ministry of women to women, the ministry of women to children in a home, and the ministry of women to men. It is this third ministry which needs clarification here. I often wonder if there are not some old men who know the secrets of good relations between men and women, just as some old women know why marriage is the greatest human experience for women. How to keep a wife contented would be wonderful wisdom for men to pass on from generation to generation. Families might become famous for producing superior husbands. The Adams family has been considered outstanding in the choice of wives. America will become a mature nation when families produce a standard of excellence by which to insure the quality of succeeding generations.

[5] *Op. cit.,* pp. 163, 164.

A woman loves the short period in her life when she is a bride. For a little while nothing else is important except that she gives pleasure to a man and in so doing pleases herself. A man would like her to be a bride always and there is no reason why she should not be. This is a situation in which it is not necessary to give up being one thing in order to become something else. It is the complexity of a woman's life which destroys her.

Could it be that men are so fearful of losing their brides that they do not wish to think seriously of a woman's work? As a wife a woman may be more charming without an education. The ministry of wives to men lies in the realm of affection. Women are the attentive audience, the source of praise, the tender critic. A man counts on his wife for loyalty when the world misunderstands him; one person who knows the best he has in him. Returning home a man finds rest in the presence of a loving wife. A woman ministers to the needs of her husband by keeping her life free, under no direction but her own so she may give any time she likes to her husband. Being the person she is means more than all the work she will ever do. To remain a bride to one's husband while using one's ability and education up to the limits of the highest standard possible in rearing the next generation requires a neat capacity for doubling. Women must know who they are before they can know what their duties are. The brief quotation at the head of this chapter is part of a longer quotation which, if understood by those in charge of the curricula of colleges, might produce an academic change as great as any produced by Eliot in his lifetime.

The great majority of women go out into the world to a single occupation. The married women bear and rear children; and a great many unmarried women bring up the children of others. An immense majority of women go into that one occupation. Because that single occupation has not been regarded as an intellectual occupation, I venture to think that this is one of the greatest mistakes civilized men and women have committed. The one great occupation there is in the world for people by the million. It calls and calls loudly—and often in vain—for carefully trained mental powers, as well as great moral powers.

When I remember the young mother who had forgotten she was a bride on that day twenty-seven years ago when she heard a very great man speak in Phillips Brooks House on "Marriage, the Greatest Event in Life," I stand amazed that he was able to tell her what it means to a man to have a loving wife. He planted the seed of an idea which has grown through the years. He told her it was more important to a man to be married to the right woman than to have anything else, for he cannot succeed without her. This chapter is the fruit of the seed sown by the ex-President of Harvard in the mind of a young woman, the wife of an inconspicuous graduate student, who has now allowed her the privilege of writing a chapter for his book.

CHAPTER IV

Responsible Fatherhood

And did not the eldest then rule among them, because
with them government originated in the authority of
a father and mother, which of all sovereignties is the
most just?

PLATO, *Laws,* III

ONE of the greatest of blessings which can come to any
normal child is the existence of two parents. There
are, of course, numerous persons who grow to splendid
maturity without this advantage, but they are forced to
overcome a serious handicap in the process. The mother
and the father are both helpful to the child and to the
home as a whole, partly because they are different, psychologically as well as physically. The importance of the
father in the home does not rest upon the absurd belief
that men and women ought to play the same role, but
rather on the recognition that their roles are different,
complementary and equally necessary.

The home, if rightly constituted, is a place in which the
woman becomes more womanly and the man becomes
more manly. It is a good thing for a man to know that he
is a man, for a woman to know that she is a woman, and

for a child to know that he is a child. A great deal of unhappiness results when the child fails to recognize his position and becomes rude or disrespectful, when the woman tries to be a pseudo-man, despising her own unique capacities, and when the man fails to rise to the responsibilities which the headship of a household entails.

In late years there has been popular acceptance of the notion that the father is just another fellow around the house, almost wholly devoid of honorable status and not even primarily responsible for the financial support of the family. The result of this heresy is bad for all concerned. Women are cheated if their husbands do not take real leadership, and children are cheated even more. Moral anarchy, even when it is disguised as democracy, does not bring happiness to the persons involved in the enterprise.

It is a wise woman who refuses to relieve her husband of the main financial responsibility of supporting the family. Sometimes the bolder policy brings in less money temporarily, but the deeper rewards are likely to come by permitting the husband to perform a task in which both he and his children can take legitimate pride. It is only when the recognition of male headship, as expressed in the Biblical story of creation, is fully accepted by both partners to a marriage that the true dignity not only of manhood, but also of wifehood is appreciated. The beauty of a woman's character appears most normally, not when she becomes the boss, but when she is truly what the Bible calls a *helpmeet*. This point is vividly illustrated by Dr. Harry Emerson Fosdick's now famous tribute to his wife, on the occasion of his retirement from Riverside Church.

He had been puzzled all his life, he said, by the fact that, on the whole, women have not accomplished as much in a public way as has been accomplished by men. Why is this true? Obviously the brains of women are as good and perhaps better than the brains of men. Yet the sober truth is that there have been relatively few women in the list of composers, artists, scientists and statesmen. "At last," said Dr. Fosdick, "I know the answer. No woman ever had a *wife*!"

As we try to understand the father's role in family life, the first thing to say is that the man's place is in the home. Of course he cannot always be there, but he must be there whenever he can. Naturally the normal father must put a great deal of time and energy into making a living and producing something of excellence in his public vocation, but his public contribution becomes a poor thing if it rules out his adequacy in his family vocation. Both must be seen as important and both must be managed in such a way that they help each other. It is especially tragic for a man to give so much time and energy to his public work that his wife and children seldom see him, and further that the bits of time he gives them are spoiled by his being tired and easily exasperated. It is hard for a father to know how deeply little children want their father's undivided time and attention. It is not fair for children always to have to compete with the newspaper. A common and touching scene on the railway train is that in which the child begs to sit with his daddy, the request being a measure, in most instances, of the child's unsatisfied hunger for this kind of companionship. The first thing, then, that a father can do for his home is to *be there*, when possible, and to give his undivided attention to those for whose existence he is responsible and who need his affection more desperately than he knows. The father who builds up the ritual of going with his children, regularly, just before bedtime, for a kitchen snack may be creating a bond of incalculable strength.

It is a sobering experience to see the bitterness of young people, sometimes of college age, who feel that they have been cheated in that their parents have never given them adequate time. This is particularly true when both parents have lived public lives and the children have been given a steady diet of boarding school in the winter, with camp in the summer, but no real home life. The fact that such people often have had plenty of money is no substitute for what is so sorely missed. It is in such ways that parents frequently pay a higher personal price for worldly success than they at first realize or than the world knows. The children of parents in modest circumstances are, for these reasons, usually more fortunate.

Having said that the father must be at home, whenever he can, we must go on to state the balancing truth that the other members of the family must, at times, be willing to make personal sacrifices, because of the father's public work. It is good for the children to know what their father is doing, to understand some of the severe demands upon his energy, and to be willing, part of the time, to forego, for this reason, joys they would like to experience. Unless the order of the world changes radically, millions of men must be out of their homes a good part of every week and some must be absent for large blocks of time. This is true of those who work on the sea, of those who are traveling salesmen and of many in government service, to mention only three areas of work. In such situations the mother must limit her own desires to be away from home, if the family is to be held together at all, and likewise the children must learn to accept their father's absence without undue self-pity. It is a good thing for children to learn, as early as possible, that life is seldom easy and that few true solutions are simple.

The good father will not only give time to his home, when he can, but he will make it a source of pride, usually superior in this regard to his work in the world. At the same time that a doctor was made president of the American Medical Association, his son was accepted in Phi Beta Kappa, and his friends noticed that he took far more satisfaction in the latter honor than in the former. Indeed, the man who, after he has a family, is still putting his main emphasis on his own personal ambition and advancement, is revealing his own failure to mature. Personal ambition may be necessary for the young, but it is increasingly unlovely in those of older years.

Since the father is human he is bound to make mistakes, and these he ought to admit to all concerned. The task of being a parent is so difficult that nobody does a perfect job of it. Every couple makes some wrong decisions, with the result that many children are very bitter, but much of this bitterness could be avoided or overcome if failures were frankly admitted. There will be failures in the family vocation, as in any other, but there is not much likelihood of bitterness on the part of children if they know very well that their parents look upon home life as a sacred calling and not a mere adjunct to public service. Then the parents will see their joint task as one which requires a vast amount of imagination as well as self-discipline.

The wise parent will be very attentive to see what it is that children desire. One of the strongest of the child's desires is to be *proud* of his parents. He wants this more than he wants money and even more than he wants time. He wants to know that others admire the ones he loves. Therefore the father who makes a public disgrace of his life or appears in a ridiculous light before his child's friends is making a very deep wound. It is right that a parent should ask frequently, in regard to some proposed course of action, "Will this make my child proud of me or ashamed of me?" This is a point very easy for mothers to forget, but they do so at great peril. The mother who neglects her own appearance, in order to give a better costume to her daughter, is undoubtedly doing so out of affection, but the affection is usually misguided, because what the daughter wants is that her mother should be admired by the daughter's contemporaries. It is often obvious that students are very nervous when their parents visit school or college. They are afraid their parents will do or say something to disgrace the family. This is one of the good reasons why parents should continue their intellectual development and should watch their modes of speech, which are so revealing to strangers. The parent makes the mistake, frequently, of concentrating on the child, when he would help the child more if he would concentrate upon himself. The parent must guard, accordingly, against the danger of too much self-sacrifice. If the sacrifice is obvious it defeats its purpose. Much as we help those whom we love by performing services for them, we help them more by being composed and happy persons. More good is done in personal relations by the habit of happiness than by obvious deeds of kindness.

It is always wrong for the child to become so much the center of the home that he is made to believe that the home revolves around him. He needs to know that both his father and his mother have lives of their own and that they are not his personal servants. He needs also to know that his father and his mother are lovers, quite apart from their relationship to him. It is the father's responsibility to make the child know that he is deeply in love with the child's mother. There is no good reason why all evidence of affection should be hidden or carried on in secret. A child who grows up with the realization that his parents are lovers has a wonderful basis of stability. This does not mean that they always agree in his presence or that all is sweetness and light. Some open controversy may actually be beneficial, providing the child has the emotional security which comes from knowing that the underlying affection is nowise disturbed. A father is harming his child, and particularly his daughter, if, in his love for her, he allows her to suppose that his love for her mother is in any way less than his love for her.

In the changing Western household the problem of joint housework is increasingly important and must be faced. Certainly we have outgrown the notion, once common in many areas, that there must be such a sharp division of labor that a man, when his day's work is done, never deigns to do any domestic labor at all. We have so far discarded this pattern that the danger now lies on the other side. It is, of course, wrong for a man to sit in his own house and be waited upon by an already overtired wife, but it is equally wrong for a man to work hard all day, at some demanding task, and then have all his home hours taken up in making beds or sweeping floors. It is important to know that there are two errors to avoid and it is certainly not the part of wisdom to cure one evil by producing another.

It is a very wise thing for a modern father, whenever his work in the world permits it, to have some task at home which he does regularly as his contribution to the total family life. This is wise, not only because it takes burdens from others by mutual sharing, but also because fellowship can be deepened thereby. This is particularly true when the father and children can do some work together regularly. In some homes the father, with the help of the children, takes over regularly the responsibility of preparing the family breakfast. This not only gives the mother an added and often much-needed rest, but draws the father and his children together. These hours of common work are often remembered with deep gratitude in subsequent years.

However good it may be for the father to take some responsibility for domestic work, we must resist at all points the increasingly popular notion that the father and mother should have *equal* responsibility. Not only is this unfair to the hard-working man; it is far more unfair to the woman. It is unfair to the woman because it takes away all sense that she has a sphere of importance, in which excellence can be developed, intelligence employed, and responsibility felt. The equal sharing of housework is a corollary of feminism and, as such, involves the fatal flaw of all feminism in that it makes women resist being women.

There is something better than the old-fashioned pattern of *no* housework on the father's part and the new-fashioned pattern which makes the father a household servant. This is the wonderfully sane notion that the man can *help* without in any degree lessening the woman's responsibility. If we take from the mother the notion that she is the queen of her little kingdom we are taking away her most legitimate source of pride, we are adding to her frustration and we are harming the total family life. Just as there is something better than either bachelorhood or polygamy, so there is something vastly better for a man's life than the role of the pampered male or than the role of the servant in the house. That this third way is possible and vastly rewarding is our own experience and the experience of many other families.

What we must do is to make the home more important as a center of family operations. The home always withers when it is chiefly a place where clothing is changed between outside engagements and a minimum of housework is grudgingly done by all concerned. It is a shame when it is assumed that all creative work is done in places removed from the home base. Perhaps more can be done by thoughtful fathers to bring part of their daily work into the family circle. Certainly the current notion of the wisdom of a sharp division between time spent at work and time spent at home is far from self-evident. It is good for children to know at firsthand the work their fathers do and it is even better if they can have some share in it. Even very small children often obtain great satisfaction from putting stamps on letters, running necessary errands, answering the telephone and doing other small tasks which make them feel like partners in the family business.

We are often amazed at the great size of old-fashioned farm homes, but our surprise is only a measure of the degree to which we have made the home a shadow of its former self. For the country family of our grandparents' day the house was not merely a place to eat and sleep; it was also a place to *work*. It was a place to render lard, to make pickles, to process milk, to stitch quilts, to braid rugs. The home was workshop, school, church and club, all in one. No doubt there were many drawbacks about such a home, and we must resist any tendency to take a sentimentally rosy view of it, but the central idea was wonderfully sound. Life had wholeness; it did not suffer from the disease of abstraction. Work and worship and play and love-making went on in the same institution. Consequently, it was a home rather than a rooming house.

To bridge the gap between the two worlds of work and of domicile is one of our major tasks, and it is not easy. It is difficult, not merely because of the inherent economic and geographical problems which urbanization and industrialization involve, but also because the very idea of a home as a place of work is foreign to us. If we keep this in mind we can do something about it. Many men who now rent offices could, if they would, bring far more of their work under the family roof and begin, consequently, to restore some of the sense of wholeness. We may be surprised to learn at what an early age children may profit from being allowed to share in family problems, including financial ones, and those having to do with the family business or vocation.

An example of how children may be included, with personal profit, in family transactions may be illustrated by the purchase of such a valued article as a piano. It is not enough to tell the child what the piano costs in money. That may mean much or little, depending upon the child's former experience. But if the cost is translated into hours or days or months of her father's labor, the child may understand. The game of buying the instrument a key or two at a time may be enjoyable to all and certainly protects the child from the vice of easy or self-indulgent acceptance of favors. Likewise, if each child has an allowance, one parent and the children can join together with enormous satisfaction in buying a gift for the other parent. The child may not be able to buy his father a watch chain, but his life is dignified by the fact that he buys an inch of it.

In the past, some fathers have taken a certain pride in never disclosing their financial situation to their children, but whenever this has occurred it has certainly been a mistake. It is hard to see that any harm can be done by a frank sharing of knowledge of transactions as soon as the child is able to understand. When a house is purchased it is good for a child to know what a mortgage is and how the mortgage is paid. He then feels something of the nature of the load his parents carry and he has the joy of being in some sense a partner. It was delightful, in one home, to hear the question, "Is this your house?" answered by an eight year old girl with the disarming reply, "It *will* be in eighteen years."

The task of buying a home is often a very burdensome one for parents in close financial circumstances, but it is important to realize that the benefits in the realm of intangibles are often immense. Children need a sense of security and of stability and the sense of owning a home is a great contribution to this end. The evils of uprootedness in family life are so great that we must oppose them with all our power. Children who are moved from house to house and from school to school can hardly emerge from the ordeal without obvious and permanent harm. A family makes few serious connections unless it is, in some sense, settled. Why attend a church or participate in community social life, many ask, if they are to be somewhere else next year. The ownership of a home, however modest, is the most direct way in which parents can give their children a sense of permanence. A great deal of the dignity of life lies in the glory of the notion of "dwelling."

The principle of sharing in creative enterprises can be applied in a host of particular ways. One of these is some kind of building operation. Though this valuable opportunity is, unfortunately, not open to all, there are millions of families in our country which might, with a little imagination, do some family building. For some fortunate ones this can be a summer cabin, but it need not be; it might be a garage or a playhouse. For years we have felt that one of our happiest enterprises came one summer with boys aged seven and twelve. We had a small sum of money which could have been used to send these boys to camp, but we decided, instead, at their strong insistence, to use the same money to buy boards and cement and shingles to make possible a four-bunk cabin in the back garden. The construction took several weeks and much ingenuity on the part of the boys, but it provided the basis of one of the most fortunate summers of their lives. They had a chance to show what they could do and they felt that it was truly a family enterprise, because we helped where heavy work was required, yet allowed all the major decisions to be made by the young builders themselves.

For others great family satisfaction may come by common work in gardening, especially if something creative is undertaken from time to time. Usually the mere tending of flowers and lawn is not enough, for there is always the boy who may ask, "Daddy, why should gardening be my hobby just because it is yours?" But if father and son decide together to build a new stone wall, to use a bulldozer in making a new level to the lawn or to install a sprinkler system, the resultant partnership may be highly productive.

One of the chief problems which any modern urban faces is that of helping to provide beneficent and useful work for his growing sons. Many a man who profited by hard work in youth now fails to help his own boy have the same or a similar opportunity for development. This is particularly true of men who grew up on farms and now live successful lives in the cities. Much of the problem is inherent in the situation rather than accidental or temporary, because so much of the work on the farm is obviously necessary, whereas many city jobs for boys seem to be arranged for their effect upon the boys, who are bright enough to know that this is the case. The boy's work in the country is serious because everyone knows that the cows have to be milked, that the chickens have to be fed and that the weeds have to be cut, if there is to be any crop. In the city there are a few serious jobs, like the delivery of newspapers, but there do not seem to be enough to go around. Accordingly thousands of big boys spend their free time in dangerous idleness. We do not have any perfect answer to this problem, but it is something to recognize its seriousness and to employ our parental imagination upon it. In any case it is generally possible to arrange for work in summers. The principle to keep in mind is that the work, in order to be effective, ought not to be merely what is known as *made* work. To achieve the desired end it must be genuine.

Important as work is, it is not all of life. There is also play and it is likewise a potential good. Every satisfactory family life includes some period of vacation for all and it is a sign of progress that so many great industries now make this a part of their total plan for their workers. Many factories now shut down for two entire weeks. Even farmers take real vacations, though the practice was once rare, and we may be sure that there is something of this nature for almost every economic level. Those who take seriously their responsibility as parents will consider carefully how vacation experiences may be used to cement family affection. This is especially important for busy men who live the kind of lives in which their children are often starved for their companionship. Perhaps these men would be wise to use the vacation period as one of family companionship to which the children can look expectantly all year. If a child can know that for two weeks every summer he can be continuously with his father whenever he desires, he can bear with better patience a great deal of deprivation and loneliness at other times of the year. The busier a man is in public life the more important it is that there be some time in the year when, from the point of view of his children, he is not busy at all. The growth in family solidarity provided by two or three weeks in the wilds, far from the bondage of the telephone, may be greater than in all the rest of the year combined. It is neither necessary nor wise that a man should be always at the call of his children, but it is both necessary and wise that he be thus available at *some* time.

Vacation scenes can also be important in family life in that they serve as a binding element as the children grow older and have children of their own. With modern industrial and business life as it is, married brothers and sisters may see almost nothing of one another during the regular year, but vacation times, if carefully planned with this purpose in mind, may become occasions of producing something very precious. There are still, in spite of our uprootedness, a few big families in which the married children can gather under the patriarchal roof, perhaps once a week. Thus a famous Baltimore doctor and his wife had, for years, twenty or thirty of their family for dinner each Sunday, and the resultant solidarity was grand to see. We have to face the fact that this sort of experience is impracticable for many modern persons, but we are wise if we get as near to it as our conditions permit. The lack of relatives near by is part of the price we pay for our industrial civilization.

We usually assume today that family enterprises, uniting the father and sons in a single co-operative work, are something from the past, but there are opportunities that we miss because we lack the idea. Recently a man in middle life changed his work and studied law so that he could practice with his lawyer son. The happiness of these two in their work is something very encouraging to observe. We cannot all be as fortunate as the Schimmel Brothers in their excellent chain of hotels which they operate together, but lesser ventures might be possible if more families could have the idea and would try. It is a shame for brothers and sisters to bring up their families in widely separated cities when this is not absolutely necessary. In any case most young people would be wise, in determining their location, to remember how beneficent family proximity may be. This ought never to be the only or even the major consideration in choosing a domicile, but it ought to be given real weight in any serious choice. What is the use of always being far removed from those whom we love if this is not really a necessity?

There are many ways in which family solidarity may be genuine, even when geographical proximity is impossible. One of these is a sense of financial responsibility among the different members. There are families in which, especially among the brothers, it is specifically understood that each brother stands ready and willing to help the children of the others if necessity arises. This is a marvelous kind of insurance and a great comfort to any man who realizes how difficult it is to have really adequate commercial insurance. It is an extension of the concept of unlimited liability which is intrinsic to the idea of the family. A wise father will encourage among his children this sense of responsibility for one another.

One of the greatest weaknesses in modern family life consists in the breakdown of discipline which is involved in the loss of authority. Nearly all observers are worried by the outbreak of violence and lawlessness among the very young, so that we are beginning to use the phrase "The Revolt of the Children."[1] The number of young offenders is so large that we are no longer shocked when we see their faces pictured in the newspapers. These faces, according to a perceptive observer, "do not always look brutish and savage, but they do look lonely, sullen and proud." Something of a very serious nature has gone wrong with these young lives, though they have not always come from what we call broken homes. In the case of a group of teen-age girls, engaged in a concerted plan of shoplifting, we are specifically told that they come from normal homes, but this means that something has gone wrong at a deep level, even in those homes in which divorce or separation has not occurred.

Much of our trouble lies in philosophical confusion, especially about such great ideas as equality and freedom.

[1] An article with this title appeared in *The Listener*, April 23, 1953.

Equality is often claimed by the young as their right, and interpreted as the notion that one person's opinion is as valuable as another's, even if the one is sixteen and ignorant, whereas the other is sixty and experienced. Personal respect is out of date. Many features in our current life, including educational tendencies of wide popularity, encourage the adolescent to suppose that he does not need to look up to anyone, and particularly not to his parents. The widespread loss of simple courtesy, which allows young people to be rude in criticism of their elders, may seem to some to be simply bad manners, but it may be, in reality, a symptom of deep moral disorder.

In the older family life, which many are belatedly beginning to appreciate, the sense of order was inherent, and for the children this was psychological good fortune. Perhaps the parents did not *make* the rules, but they expressed them, and the children usually knew what the rules were. What the child experienced, then, was the extremely beneficent combination of an impersonal order with the personal sense of forgiveness when infractions occurred. When the idea of the family has withered, as it has in so many areas today, there is no sin because there is no order, and there is no forgiveness because there are no elders and betters to do the forgiving. Nothing is accepted as having been given or bestowed, but all privileges are accepted ungraciously as natural rights. This is bound to lead to moral confusion, for it is essential to the good life that things should be given and received. The art of receiving requires as much moral development as does the art of giving, and may be more difficult to achieve.

Much of our present failure in family life is the fault of parents who have adopted uncritically a false and empty notion of freedom. The more critical we become the more we realize that freedom, far from being a necessary good, is highly ambiguous and variable in value. The freedom which means the absence of all restraint is far from valuable and leads straight to brutishness of many kinds. The fortunate child is not the one who grows up in a world which has neither rules nor boundaries. The child needs boundaries, with an area of freedom within the boundaries, if he is to develop any sense of security. The playground is more enjoyable in the long run if it has a fence around it. The child needs parents to make some big decisions which relieve the very young from burdens for which their experience has not prepared them. The immense value of rules and regulations is that they relieve the immature individual of the intolerable burden of responsibility involved in the practice of unlimited choice.

The modern father, if he is to contribute his rightful share to the reconstruction of our total society and fulfill his parental vocation, must accept the burden of authority. Within his little kingdom he must take a position of responsibility and thus help to overcome the prevalent notion of moral anarchy. He must resist the superficial notion of equality. He ought to know more than his child knows; he ought to be wiser; he ought to make decisions that are unchallenged. Then when he wisely gives more freedom and helps to develop initiative by degrees, these are more likely to be appreciated than abused. He will have the grace to forgive as well as the courage to admit failure on occasion, but he will never forget that the role of father is different from the role of child. He will not abdicate.

It is not likely that any modern father will make the mistakes depicted in *The Barrets of Wimpole Street*. The father of Mrs. Browning undoubtedly failed by too great a stress on his parental authority, as the modern father fails by too little stress. Somewhere between these two extremes there is surely a middle ground which encourages the individuality of the child, but also gives the child the necessary emotional security of the consciousness of a hand that is strong while it is loving. The good father will always resist the temptation to try to cast the son in his own mold, particularly in the choice of a profession, and, as the child becomes a man, the father will recognize this fact. But if affection and mutual respect are maintained nearly all problems of this nature can be solved.

The father's task does not come to an end when the child marries or leaves the parental roof. Indeed, the period of early married life is a period of very great need, both of counsel and of money. The idea that parents should support their children until marriage, and then do no more, is as absurd as it is widespread. The young man may need more help during his first year *out* of college than he needs *in* college. If the parents can afford it, it is far better to give funds to help young couples to get on their feet than to leave the money as an inheritance after death. If the young couple needs a car and cannot afford it, the solvent father is wise to use his resources to make the ownership possible. This facilitates earlier marriage and is good for all concerned.

The tasks and responsibilities of parenthood are so great that it seems almost impossible for anyone to succeed in performing them. God, we often think, should have given parents more brains than have been given to any. Yet, in spite of the difficulty, and in the midst of failure, many families are being held together in a wonderful way. In this lies hope for our troubled yet exciting generation.

CHAPTER V

The Sources of Family Strength

> On the whole, ought I not to rejoice that God was
> pleased to give me such a father: that from earliest
> years I had the example of a real man of God's own
> making continually before me? Let me learn of *him*.
> Let me write my books as he built his houses, and
> walk as blamelessly through this shadow world.
>
> THOMAS CARLYLE

I T IS not necessary to invent a religious program for the
home, because the home is intrinsically a religious institution. Sometimes the religion inculcated in the family is
bad religion, self-centered and contemptuous of others,
sometimes it is a secular religion, as in the case of Marxism,
but in any case the home is the place where most people receive their earliest and deepest convictions about that to
which they are committed. Since it is a great part of wisdom
about life to learn to do well what cannot be avoided, we
must learn all that we can from one another about the ways
in which the home may rightly perform its inevitable task.

There has been in late years a fashionable trend in the
direction of leaving children entirely free, so far as their

deepest faith is concerned, with the thought that they will then choose for themselves when they reach the age of maturity. Superficially this approach has a certain attractiveness, since it seems to respect the individuality of the child so much that he is set free from all indoctrination. Actually, however, the idea is one of the most fallacious that can be imagined. The supposed freedom from indoctrination does not and cannot really occur, because the child is living in the real world all of the time and drawing conclusions on the basis of the evidence. Usually this amounts to a very strong indoctrination in a secular view of life. The child is wise enough to know that parents who do not feel keenly enough about any living faith to pass it on to their children do not have any worth mentioning. They know very well that the parents do not leave them the complete freedom to choose about matters they consider important; they are not told to wait and make up their minds later about drugs or germs or scientific knowledge. The child senses, therefore, that the parents consider religion insignificant, which means that they are not committed to it, which usually means that the children follow the same line. What looked like a fair throw was actually made with loaded dice. Those who have had very many dealings with these children of free choice know that the outcome is often very far from being what the supposedly sophisticated parents naïvely hoped.

There is a second reaction to this refusal to indoctrinate which is becoming more common and which has in it, in spite of bitterness, an element of hope. It is not uncommon now for children, at the end of adolescence, to revolt against the emptiness of their parents' homes. A boy complains that he has not been fairly treated, that he has been brought up wholly without any acquaintance with the rich resources of the Bible and without the practice of prayer. We once thought of revolt as always revolt against piety, but many modern youngsters, if they are to revolt at all, now have to revolt in the other direction.

Fortunately, there is something better than the indoctrination which the emancipated have feared or than the secular emptiness which has commonly been substituted for it. What is possible is the kind of home in which a living faith is more caught than taught, because it is the unstated groundwork of all that is done and said. In such a home, as in any truly religious institution, the chief influences are unconscious, particularly on the part of the young whose lives are molded thereby. We do not know, usually, by what particular forces our minds are guided in certain definite directions, but we realize finally that our standards *are* set. The strongest incentives in the development of the characters of children often come, not from direct and specific instruction, but from example and from unargued assumptions. Argument about the wisdom of attendance at public worship is almost trivial in comparison with the long-time effect of a steady habit of attendance on the part of all members of the family from the time before the child can remember. The child's good fortune lies, in great measure, in being a part of an ongoing little society in which a high sense of both integrity and reverence is expected, but not debated.

The power of expectancy in the lives of children is something which it is almost impossible to exaggerate. It is far more important for a child to grow up in a family in which it is always expected that he will keep his promises than for him to hear a lecture on promise keeping. It is far better to grow up thinking of prayer as a normal and expected part of living than to be told to pray. Herein lies the terrible fallacy of those parents who, having decided that it is a good thing for their boys and girls to get some religious instruction, send them to the church school to get it. The fact that there is no prayer in the home is almost sure to convince the alert child that prayer is something for special places and for special times, having little to do with normal and nonecclesiastical living. Perhaps he will think of it as the professional job of religious experts.

It was central to the very idea of the ancient Hebrew law that it be made pervasive in ordinary existence. The divine order was not something for a separate sphere, but was part of the air men breathed and part of the way they worked. This is the point of the great and moving declaration in the following words:

And these words, which I command thee this day, shall be in thine heart: And thou shalt teach them diligently unto thy children, and shalt talk of them when thou sittest in thine house, and when thou walkest by the way, and when thou liest down, and when thou risest up. And thou shalt bind them for a sign upon thine hand, and they shall be as frontlets between thine eyes. And thou shalt write them upon the posts of thy house, and on thy gates.[1]

[1] Deut. 6:6-9.

One important way in which this ancient wisdom may be made applicable today is for the religious experience of the child to begin before he is able to understand its meaning. A four year old sitting on his father's lap and hearing the Psalms in the rich poetry of the Authorized Version may misunderstand the meaning of many of the words, but that is no reason for denying him the experience. He may secure from it a sense of nobility in expression that may affect his mature taste years later and, what is more significant, he may begin to feel something akin to genuine reverence. Later when he listens to stories from Genesis he may love them so that he is unwilling for his mother to stop at the end of the chapter. Certainly there is no necessity at all for the spread of the notion that such reading must be dull and forbidding.

There is no doubt that specific religious instruction by a church organization may have great value, but most of its value depends upon its support by a favorable climate in the homes from which the children come and to which they return. Fortunately, we do not need to choose between religion in the church and religion in the home, since both work together easily, but if choice were necessary it is clear where the priority would lie. The absence of prayer at home is more damaging than is absence of prayer at Sunday School. What is necessary is that the ordinary child grow up with the notion that religion is not at all queer or strange, but is a normal part of normal living.

There is no way to overestimate the power of a sense of belonging, as it affects young persons. Family tradition may not always be good, but it always makes a difference.

The Robinson boy soon learns, as he watches his father, that the Robinsons are a particular kind of people and that he is expected to be one of them. There are some things so low that people of his kind don't stoop to them and this realization is far more effective than overt demands. The child tries to demonstrate what he essentially *is*. Perhaps the one influence which a boy finds hardest to resist is that which comes when he is told, "Be a man." What he is *potentially*, begins to determine what he becomes in *actuality*. There is a sense in which the family is made by the individuals which constitute it, but there is a far deeper sense in which the individuals are made by the family.

We usually think of pride as a sin, but it need not always be so. There is a kind of pride that is wonderfully beneficent in the human enterprise and this is particularly clear when we consider family pride. Many a person has been strengthened in hard places by the desire not to let his family down. As individuals we are weak at best, but we can be strengthened by the sense of an honorable background. Young people, faced by sexual temptation, may rightly be helped by the keen realization that they and their family have a reputation to maintain. Even grandfather's portrait may be a powerful incentive to right living. In a similar way young people may be strengthened to accept unpopular courses or stand against general hysteria if they have a sense of family tradition behind them. It is a rewarding sight to see a young person refuse to share in racial antagonism because he belongs to a family of people who are queer in that they always seek to respect each person, of whatever race, in the light of his inherent dignity as a human being.

We are helped, in this connection, by the fact that a good many persons of strong character have been able to remember and to tell others of the influences most formative in their early lives. Outstanding in this regard is *Memoirs of Childhood and Youth* by Albert Schweitzer, and three books by the late Rufus M. Jones, *A Boy's Religion from Memory, Finding the Trail of Life,* and *A Small Town Boy.* What were the early influences which helped these two men to develop into characters of such power for good? What did their parents do to start them on the road to that combination of inner devotion and creative human service which so many now admire?

Dr. Schweitzer is convinced that the very best thing his devout family did for him was to expect him, even as a very young boy, to share in a dignified and serious public worship of God. The following paragraph is valuable to any sincere parent who is trying to find the right way for his child:

From the services in which I joined as a child I have taken with me into life a feeling for what is solemn, and a need for quiet and self-recollection, without which I cannot realize the meaning of my life. I cannot, therefore, support the opinion of those who would not let children take part in grown-up people's services till they to some extent understand them. The important thing is not that they shall understand but that they shall feel something of what is serious and solemn. The fact that the child sees his elders full of devotion, and has to feel something of devotion himself, that is what gives the service its meaning for him.[2]

Dr. Schweitzer believes his interest in missions, the guiding interest of his adult life, was aroused in the afternoon services which he attended as a very young boy. For many Sundays in succession the boy listened as his father read the memoirs of a missionary to Africa. Let anyone who wonders whether reading to children is wasted contemplate the final effect of this early experience. In the long run the mood of prayer provides a more effective setting than does the mood of mere instruction. Prayer is the heart of religion, private religion being largely private prayer and public religion being largely public prayer. This may give pause to those parents who suppose that Sunday School is sufficient and fail to introduce their children, at an early age, to the elevating atmosphere of divine worship.

Rufus Jones' account of the atmosphere of his boyhood home in a Maine village is such as to make others envy him. He felt the power of a family tradition before he knew that he was feeling it.

I am most of all thankful for my birthplace and early nurture in the warm atmosphere of a spiritually-minded home, with a manifest touch of saintliness in it; thankful indeed that from the cradle I was saturated with the Bible and immersed in an environment of religion of experience and reality. It was a peculiar grace that I was born into that great inheritance of spiritual wisdom and faith, accumulated through generations of devotion and sacrificial love. I never can be grateful enough

[2] Albert Schweitzer, *Memoirs of Childhood and Youth* (New York: The Macmillan Company, 1931), p. 62.

for what was done for me by my progenitors before I came on the scene. They produced the spiritual atmosphere of my youth. I became heir of a vast invisible inheritance. There is nothing I would exchange for that.

What shall we say, in the light of such a glowing report, of the situation of families in which there is no such inheritance? Are they without hope? By no means. It is possible to *start* a tradition when there is none to be continued. It is a greater achievement to be an ancestor than a mere descendant. Any couple, conscious of the importance of the production of an atmosphere of reverence, can begin at once the effort to produce it.

The problem of family worship seems, in the modern world, almost insoluble. We might suppose that our labor-saving devices would give us more time for the great undertakings, but somehow they almost never do. We are well aware of the beauty of the older practice in many families, according to which the father, at the beginning or the end of the day, would read, in the presence of all, a considerable passage of Scripture, after which there would be vocal prayer, sometimes with the participation of all members of the circle. How can we do this now, with children rushing for the school bus, perhaps on different schedules, and with the father often leaving home while it is still dark on winter mornings? A few may still succeed in keeping the pattern of the family altar, but it is fruitless to try to urge it upon all. It simply will not be done. A counsel of perfection may actually be harmful since, when it seems impossible, many conclude that there is *nothing* that they can do and act accordingly.

The part of wisdom is to see what may reasonably be expected of the average modern family and emphasize that with all our power. The point at which most families could begin is grace before meat. Most families, if they really try, can have at least one unhurried and peaceful meal in the day as an entire family. If your family pattern is such that this proves to be impossible, it may be right to consider a basic change in work or location, for the common meal is central. If the one good family meal of the day can be eaten in peace and order, however simple, and if it can be preceded by prayer that is not perfunctory, a great start is already made toward making the home the beneficent religious institution which it ought always to be.

Grace before meat may take many valid forms. Sometimes it ought to be silent prayer, as all sit with heads reverently bowed, each encouraged to make his own prayer. Sometimes a grace ought to be sung or familiar words repeated. Do not suppose that the vocal prayer should be limited to the father of the house. Children as young as four or five can learn to share profitably, even by composing spontaneous prayers on the spot. On other occasions, great classics of prayer may be read with profit. It is one mark of a devout home to have near the dining table a shelf of devotional volumes, including Bible and Prayer Book. Even young children can learn to use these reverently and if the reading is not perfect we need not mind, for we remember that God has chosen what is weak in the world to shame the strong. What is of central importance is that the enterprise must always be genuine and one way of assuring this is to avoid the deadly dullness of always doing it in the same way. We must seek variety deliberately, both in materials and in participation.

The table is the center of the home! Ordinarily there are many beds, but only one *board*. The idea that a meal may be a sacred occasion is so deeply rooted in many religious traditions that it cannot be accidental or of passing significance. The forms of the sacred meal most familiar to us are the Jewish Passover and the Christian love feast, of which the Eucharist is a formalized vestige, but these are not the only examples in religious history. Of especial significance to all Christians is the fact that, according to the gospel record, the Risen Christ was recognized by the disciples at the moment that they began to share in the ordinary meal.[3] This leads to the hope that every common meal may be, if we are sufficiently sensitive, a time when we are conscious of the real presence of our Lord. Undoubtedly He is always present, but in many situations we are blind to the presence in the midst. The breaking of bread is potentially such a holy act, that it becomes the means by which we see that to which we are otherwise blind. Of this we may be sure: any child who has, day in and day out, over a period of years, shared in a genuine time of reverence at the family table, has something built into his life that he is not likely to lose, whatever periods of perplexity he may experience in subsequent years.

All the world religions have made much of the great occasions, such as seed time and harvest, as well as birth,

[3] Luke 24:31-35.

marriage and death. In its own way, a particular family can do this and inaugurate its own festivals, whether gay or solemn. The birth of a new baby may be the occasion of a tremendous spiritual experience on the part of the older brothers and sisters. And death, in the family as in the world, must be met within the context of a faith which, far from denying our grief, expresses and thereby ennobles it. In our own situation we found that, when grandfather died, the distance was too great for any of us to go to the funeral, so our little company gathered around the study fire at the same time as the funeral two thousand miles away, and we find that the experience is something for which we shall be forever grateful. The New Testament phrase, "the church that is in thy house," took on a new and vital meaning for us.

Birthdays, the start of long journeys, homecomings, graduations, new jobs, the completion of a new house—all these are the stuff of which the religion of the home may be made. Religion is not something separated from ordinary life, but the way in which common life may be made sacred. God, we believe, is not primarily interested in religion, but in *living*, not primarily in churches, but in *people*. If we can believe that a home is potentially as much a sanctuary as any ecclesiastical building can ever be, we are well on the way to the recovery of family life which our generation so sorely needs.

A spirit of common devotion may not accomplish everything, but it will work wonders. Couples who are finding terrible and perhaps justifiable fault with one another are not likely to separate if they face their problems in prayer and in the humility which prayer tends to produce. A person who understands prayer is not thereby made sentimental about the characters of others, and he is not blind to the fact of sin, but the sins of which he is most conscious are his own. There would be few divorces if the separated couples could somehow be brought to face their difficulties on their knees. The same is true of tensions between parents and children. Much is said of the way in which it is natural for young people to revolt against the religious emphasis of their parents. We are glad to make our witness, for what it is worth, that there has not been any religious revolt of our children at all. Each one has attended public worship from earliest childhood and those now adults have continued, without a break, to feel their own responsibilities. Part of this, we believe, arises from the fact that from the beginning we used the power of expectancy rather than of force. We tried to make them feel like responsible persons, even in very early years. Perhaps we have just been lucky, but we are happy about the result.

All who know anything about the Jewish religion are aware of the power that lies in the special Jewish home celebrations, especially at the beginning of the Sabbath on Friday nights. The Jewish child who sees the Sabbath lights kindled in his own home each week, while they are not kindled in the houses of many of the neighbors, is being given a deep sense of belonging to an ongoing and special tradition. Slowly, and often unconsciously, he is being given the conviction that special strength will be required of him and that he is part of an old movement of which he has a right to be proud. All who contemplate it realize that the way in which the Jews, in spite of fierce persecution, have held together as a people, is one of the great miracles of history, but the home festival is part of the explanation. Here is something which it is very hard for even organized persecution to stop. The Nazis could tear down the synagogue, but it was hard for them to stop the inauguration of the Sabbath with prayer. We understand a great deal of the genius of Judaism when we familiarize ourselves with the following prayer which is part of the meditation before the kindling of the Sabbath lights:

Father of Mercy, O continue thy lovingkindness unto me and unto my dear ones. Make me worthy to rear my children that they walk in the way of the righteous before thee, loyal to thy law and clinging to good deeds. Keep thou from us all manner of shame, grief and care; and grant that peace, light and joy ever abide in our home.

It is admittedly more difficult for those without a conscious ancient tradition to have anything equally strong, but imaginative parents may build up their own reminders, if they are willing to try. What we need to remember is that these important matters take intelligent attention and never do themselves easily. The good family life, especially in its definitely religious aspect, is something at which we must work without ceasing. One helpful practice, which many could adopt, is the use of special times for remembering the absent members of the family. If the older children are married and gone, or if some are in peculiar danger, prayer for them on the part of those remaining in the home may be particularly beneficent to all concerned.

There are, of course, many books of prayers, though not many really good ones. One of the best adapted for home use is the slender volume which Mrs. Robert Louis Stevenson brought out after her husband's death. Since it is made up of the prayers which Stevenson wrote for their household in Samoa, the domestic flavor appears on almost every page. Not many persons are sufficiently insensitive to fail to be moved and helped by a prayer like the following:

Aid us, if it be thy will, in our concerns. Have mercy on this land and innocent people. Help them who this day contend in disappointment with their frailties. Bless our family, bless our forest house, bless our island helpers. Thou who hast made for us this place of ease and hope, accept and inflame our gratitude; help us to repay, in service one to another, the debt of thine unmerited benefits and mercies, so that, when the period of our stewardship draws to a conclusion, when the windows begin to be darkened, when the bond of the family is to be loosed, there shall be no bitterness of remorse in our farewells.

Stevenson was a great writer, but he was also a simple Christian. Apparently there was nothing in the least self-conscious about his part in the family worship. It was normal to eat; it was normal to sleep; it was normal to pray. There is, in this, an important lesson which the modern men and women, who care about their families, may profitably learn. So many of us are reticent to the point of complete inarticulateness, when it comes to our faith. We become embarrassed at mention of the name of God; we are apologetic in our expressions. Sometimes we try to disguise this as humility, but the disguise is too thin to be effective. What we need is the habit of being as forthright and unapologetic about our religion as about anything else. A parent who cannot talk to a child directly and simply about God is not succeeding as a parent, whatever success he may achieve in other ways. We ought to realize that a halfhearted and stammering faith cannot be a sufficient resource in our puzzled time.

The honest parent will never claim that he knows all the answers, but, insofar as his faith is genuine, he will have some central convictions in the light of which all the puzzling questions may be faced. Here the truly marvelous approach is that of Christ when he prayed, "I thank thee, O Father, Lord of heaven and earth, that thou hast hid these things from the wise and prudent, and hast revealed them unto babes."[4] If, at the heart of all the world, there is One who, at the same time, is as tender as a good father and yet the master of the world's order, whether here or yonder, we have a faith big enough to face any difficulty. If a child raises the question of scientific evidence and natural law, as making a difficulty for prayer, the answer is that all natural law is only an expression of the divine purpose and is subsidiary to it. All that our scientific evidence can do is to find out a tiny part of the nature of the world which God has made and which His will sustains. If the child asks who made God, the honest parent should answer that the One who is truly Lord of Heaven and earth needs no one to *make* Him, since He alone is truly independent. *We* require a Maker, but our Maker does not. Even a small child, if he is old enough to ask the question, can be intellectually satisfied with this answer, providing

[4] Matt. 11:25.

the parent seems deep enough in his faith to feel sure of his central conviction that this really is God's world, all of it. One of the chief reasons why so many parents have had difficulty at this and similar points is that they have not been genuine believers themselves. It is very hard to pass on a faith which we do not ourselves possess.

Many parents today find great difficulty in guiding their children in the use of the Bible because the parents do not know how to use it themselves. The curious mistake they make lies in the supposition that understanding of the Bible can somehow come without work, whereas everyone agrees that all other noble enterprises entail hard labor. With such marvelous modern guides as *The Interpreter's Bible* and other works available to any layman, the day is long past when ordinary parents needed to feel helpless about their great religious responsibilities. Ordinary fathers and mothers, many of whom have had college educations, could carry on at home the same level of studies as is carried on in theological seminaries and many would find such studies truly exciting. One result of such study would be the ability to present children with a reasoned faith, marked alike by scientific integrity and evangelical vigor.

Each home will have to make its own experiment in religious education if the moral sag of our time is to be altered. The change cannot come by governmental fiat or even by some public educational reform. The best education is that of the laboratory and the only laboratory in which the most important lessons can be learned is that of the separated home. Some of these, such as that of the British Royal Family, can make a great difference in our civilization. There is no way to overestimate the beneficent moral effect which Queen Elizabeth and her family are having, not merely for England and the whole British Commonwealth, but for the entire Western world. Here, at the focus of admiring attention, is a scene of family happiness and fidelity which makes the too common café society of our time seem utterly shoddy by contrast. The center of attention is a really good young family, marked by fidelity, and this is a moral force beyond price.

Each little family may exert its own influence, on a smaller scale, even though it is not the center of general attention. It is sobering to go through the country by car or train and begin to contemplate the meaning of all the little houses. In most of these homes dwell one man and one woman and their little ones, all working together to achieve an honorable life. Their success almost never appears in newspapers, but perhaps it is better thus. Each little unit is striving to pay its bills, get rid of the mortgage, keep the grass cut, keep the children fed and clothed, buy new shoes, and send the children to school with regularity. No national scheme we could imagine would provide the same drive that is provided by the combination of the individual pride and affection of all these families existing separately, each as a little kingdom. In the larger community action is difficult and often slow, but in a good family there is wonderful freedom to act. Here are both initiative and independence which make the American home the bulwark of the American way. It is a good way and it will survive. We must keep the private home and we must make it better. If we have enough good homes we shall have a good world. But we shall not succeed in making them better in time unless we have the kind of motivation which a crusade makes possible. The problems of family life today are so great that they cannot possibly be solved on the merely secular level. Only something as strong as a sense of religious vocation will suffice.

If the hard-pressed men and women in the little homes, who are faced with difficulties every day, can be made to feel that they, in maintaining families, are in a crucial position, doing that which the world sorely needs and without which the world will go to pieces, they may be enabled to face their tasks with a wholly new spirit. It is the responsibility of every reader of this book to feel this sense of vocation in trying to make his own home into a place where the Christian revolution begins, and to spread this idea to as many others as possible.

Set in Linotype Baskerville
Format by John Rynerson
Manufactured by The Haddon Craftsmen, Inc.
Published by HARPER *&* BROTHERS, *New York*